KV-578-061

# GREAT EMIGRATIONS

Series Editor: Douglas Hill

# The English to New England

## Douglas Hill

GENTRY BOOKS · LONDON

First published 1975
© Douglas Hill 1975
ISBN 0 85614 021 X

Published by Gentry Books Limited
85 Gloucester Road, London SW7
Designed by Brian Roll
Printed in Great Britain by
William Clowes & Sons, Limited
London, Beccles and Colchester

# Contents

# Illustrations

# Maps

Cartography: David L. Fryer & Co.

# 1. Plymouth Company

America looks back to the seventeenth century in its birthday celebrations, but the impetus that first transplanted Englishmen to the New World's Atlantic coast grew out of that expansive, adventurous, exploratory surge which characterized the heyday of the Elizabethan age. A good many sixteenth-century notables sought to direct those bursting energies towards practical, businesslike activities in the wake of adventure—predominantly, colonization to follow up discovery. Richard Hakluyt, brilliant anthologist of other men's explorations, spoke out especially strongly about the material value and the political gains to be found in staking an English claim to the American new-found lands.

> This enterprise may stay the Spanish King from flowing over all the face of that waste firm of America, if we seat and plant there in time, in time I say.... And England possessing the purposed place of planting, Her Majesty may, by the benefit of the seat, having won good and royal havens, have plenty of excellent trees for masts, of goodly timber to build ships and to make great navies, of pitch, tar, hemp and all things incident for a navy royal, and that for no price, and without money or request. How easy a matter may it be to this realm, swarming at this day with valiant youths, rusting and hurtful by lack of employment ... to be lords of all those seas. . . .*

*It should be made clear that in all quotations from past centuries, where necessary, the spelling and punctuation (but not the vocabulary) have ben modernized. The only argument for retaining the original form would seem to be in a rather patronizing enjoyment of its quaintness; the loss of this period charm is more than compensated for by the gain in accessibility.

1

# The English to New England

Included within the general region that Hakluyt was considering in his *Discourse Concerning Western Planting* was a comparatively small stretch of rocky coastal land, jagged with harbours, lying south and west of the Bay of Fundy, north and east of the Hudson river. That area today contains the six New England states of the American Union —Connecticut, Maine, Massachusetts, New Hampshire, Rhode Island and Vermont (here listed alphabetically, rather than in any order of prominence). At various times during its colonial past, of course, the region was carved up into other divisions, which were given other names—some bestowed by the early English arrivals to those shores, those who appeared soon after Hakluyt wrote, and who tried to implement his concept of an English 'planting' in the wilderness that was to become New England.

But it seems only appropriate to begin before them with the earliest arrival of all—John Cabot, sailing out of Bristol under English colours to cross the Atlantic a few years after Columbus, anchoring his little ship off the coast of Newfoundland as the true discoverer of North America. Feats like this at the dawn of the sixteenth century ushered in those heady times when Britannia came to rule more and more waves, when English seafarers clashed with Spain and searched everywhere for treasure lands of their own, or for quick routes to the rich trade with the Orient. Cabot's find, and comparable visits shortly after by Giovanni da Verrezano and Jacques Cartier (both sailing on behalf of France), implanted the myth of a 'Northwest Passage' in the European mind. But Cabot had also brought back news of a more practical nature—fish in the seas round Newfoundland, so abundant that a basket could be lowered over a ship's side to scoop up cod from the water. In fish-hungry Catholic Europe, this plenty meant profit, and in the early 1500s the ships of every maritime nation were on the Grand Banks, hurling out their nets to the apparently inexhaustible bounty. England, France and Portugal predominated, and some of the captains moved inland as well to trade with the Indians for furs. It may have been a trivial source of profit compared to what Spain took out of her possessions to the south, which England envied enormously; but it kept the commercial paths open to our area.

The Spanish presence in the New World also led to the persistent awareness, in England, that overseas possessions would be made secure by actual human presence—that is, settlement. The first attempt at an English colony in North America was made by Sir Humphrey Gilbert, half-brother of Walter Raleigh, in the 1580s: he took formal possession of Newfoundland for the Crown, then sailed south along the coast to examine the possibilities in those regions. What he would have thought of New England remains unknown, since a monstrous storm drowned him, his ships and his colonial hopes at the same time.

Still, there were other sixteenth-century opinions of New England to be taken, if anyone had been interested. Verrezano had not cared for the weather, but had admired the abundance of naturally protected harbours and the wealth of game, fruit, nuts and other sustenance of the huge forests. (These two points would be made in the region's favour by every colonial newcomer from then on.) He had also enjoyed meeting some of the Indian tribes—for most of whom he was the first white man seen—but found a few, like those of Maine, unpleasant and hostile. Verrezano's trail-blazing reports on New England were extended by perhaps less thorough ones from Spain's Estevan Gomez (1525), from a captain attached to Cartier's expedition to Quebec (1541) who almost certainly took a look at Massachusetts Bay, and a few others through the mid-century.

So awareness of the eastern coasts of America existed at least on the fringe of the European mind in those times, and came in for more attention after Gilbert's disaster and Raleigh's abortive attempts to colonize Roanoke Island (off the coast of North Carolina), in 1585 and 1587. Then, as the Elizabethan age moved into its end-of-century glory, England's seagoing supremacy began to manifest itself less in adventurous privateering and more in expanding trade —which gave even more credibility to concepts of colonization voiced by Hakluyt and Raleigh and their ilk. Eventually those concepts, and the available knowledge of New England, led to one sea captain's decision to essay a colony there—where the Indians were reputedly more friendly than those whose antagonism made an end of Raleigh's Roanoke dream.

The captain's name was Bartholomew Gosnold, and he sailed from Cornwall in 1602 with thirty-two men including Sir Humphrey Gilbert's son Raleigh. Landing on the coast of what is now New Hampshire, they were met by an array of Indians, some of whom astonishingly carried European utensils and implements while others wore bits and pieces of European clothing—as if to underline to the expedition how numerous had been its predecessors. Moving south, Gosnold's company explored and fished off a prominent point of land and—as one of the voyagers put it—'pestered our ship so with cod fish' that they named the point Cape Cod. Gosnold planted other names which are still current, including Martha's Vineyard, given to an island south of the Cape that was immensely rich in game and berry bushes. Then, on another island nearby (then called Elizabeth's, now called Cuttyhunk), Gosnold halted his expedition and made his settlement—erecting a crude fort, planting grain and vegetables, exploring, and above all gathering sassafras. This plant was much valued as an ingredient in many remedies current then in European medicine—it was believed to be curative of nearly everything from plague to indigestion—and a shipload of it would nicely defray the costs of the colonization.

Gosnold and his company also traded with Indians from the mainland, who seemed friendly enough, and who showed no clear signs of previous contact with Europeans. But later, when Gosnold and some of the men were away gathering cedar wood, another potentially valuable cargo, two of the men left behind were inexplicably attacked by a small party of those Indians, and one of the colonists was wounded by an arrow. This disaster changed everyone's minds about New England. The twenty men who had been intended to remain behind as permanent colonists, while Gosnold and the others took the ship and cargo back to England, suddenly decided the idea was less than palatable; and their distaste for it led them to arguing about the fair division of supplies, and to other disruptive acts. Gosnold apparently lost control of his men, with the result that when the ship sailed it bore every one of the original thirty-two, while behind them the unoccupied fort and gardens of the first New England colony were left to crumble and rot.

Later European arrivals on the same shores came solely in search of profitable sassafras, fish and other commodities; colonization ideas faded for a while. In 1603 Martin Pring of Devonshire took two ships along Gosnold's route for some distance before making his way into the expanse of

Massachusetts Bay and finally Plymouth Harbour. They busily gathered sassafras and made several contacts with local Indians; but some unpleasantness arose, largely because of the sort of contemptuous and usually brutal practical joking that Europeans seemed always to like perpetrating on 'less civilized' peoples. When one of the ships set sail with its load of sassafras the Indians grew even more threatening towards those who remained; and when they finally fired the woods Pring felt the need for discretion, loaded his cargo and crew and sailed away to England.

By then several moneyed and a few titled gentlemen had begun to take an increasing interest in the sowing of Englishmen in the region Pring visited. One of these top people with the colonizing urge was the Earl of Southampton, his freedom and wealth restored by James I after the old queen's death. In 1605 he came together with the wealthy Sir Ferdinando Gorges, military governor of Plymouth in Devon, who was to be the most determined and devoted financier of New England colonial ventures in the early seventeenth century. They equipped Captain George Weymouth to follow in Pring's steps, and so in the spring of that year another little English ship nosed into the bays of the Maine coast, its crew as usual admiring the proliferating fish, game and fruit, and finding a superb harbour called St George's.

Also as usual, the local Indians discovered their presence and made contact, which seems at first to have been friendly and interesting to both sides. Then Weymouth's men apparently became nervous, by virtue of being outnumbered —though some historians do not give them this benefit of the doubt, asserting that they simply became unpleasant and avaricious. In any case, five Indians were lured on board the ship and imprisoned—perhaps as hostages, at first, but finally to be carried off to England when Weymouth sailed for home. It seems an unnecessarily cruel act, akin to slaving, though at least the Indians were not badly treated. Sir Ferdinando Gorges took three into his home to put them through a 'civilizing' process.

Gorges also began contemplating more far-reaching adventures. And not before time: by then the flag of France was encroaching onto New England soil, as Samuel de Champlain continued his systematic and tireless explorations from New France on the St Lawrence river. Later in

1605 Champlain was in fact to visit Massachusetts, locating many of the great harbours such as Plymouth and Boston, then finally slipping north again to choose Passamaquoddy Bay as a suitable site for a settlement. But bad weather and worse terrain soon defeated this French attempt at colonization; when Champlain removed his colony to a location in what is now Canada's Nova Scotia, he left the way open again for New England to acquire that name.

In those early years of James I's reign, Britain was noticing that other maritime nations were outstripping her in the accumulation of colonies, so useful commercially as sources of raw materials and markets for manufacturers —and also, some began to see, as places to which to drain surplus manpower in the frequent periods of depression and unemployment. Those years were such a period; and out of this need men like Southampton and Gorges petitioned for some royal blessing on their colonization dreams. In 1606 their requests bore fruit: a royal charter brought into being two 'companies of adventurers', as so many seventeenth-century trading-cum-colonization companies were romantically called. One was known as the London Company, but sometimes as the Virginia Company, since its attentions focused on the region from North Carolina to New Jersey. The other was the Plymouth Company, concerned with the region from New Jersey to the northern tip of Maine.

Gorges was a principal backer of the Plymouth Company, as was Sir John Popham, Lord Chief Justice of England. (It is interesting to see the latter investing in this company: remember that Sir Walter Raleigh had held a 'patent' for the lands on the east coast of America, which had had to be voided before the two new companies could be formed. Popham had presided at the trial that destroyed Raleigh and sent him to the Tower.) Out went three of their ships in 1606, one of them carrying two of Weymouth's kidnapped Indians to act as pilots; another of them was captained by Martin Pring again. But none of these established a colony; that distinction came to a *fourth* Plymouth company ship in 1607 commanded by George Popham, one of the Justice's relatives, and Raleigh Gilbert, who had been with Gosnold.

They retraced Weymouth's path along the coast, and in August came to rest in the mouth of what is now the Ken-

nebec river of Maine. There they formally declared themselves a British colony, and there they erected a fort and
a storehouse, while engaging at the same time in diffident
contacts with the Indians. (They had taken another of
Weymouth's captive Indians with them, and were upset
when he promptly vanished into the wilderness with his
kinfolk, depriving them of his services as guide and interpreter.) Gilbert managed a few exploratory trips into
the surrounding vicinity, one of which nearly led to a
conflict with an unfriendly Indian band from upriver.
Work proceeded well, with the fort (or stockade) finished
and some fifty houses built within it. In the words of a
fragmentary and limited contemporary account of the
colony, all things were 'in good forwardness, and many
kinds of furs obtained from the Indians by way of trade,
good store of sarsparilla [sassafras?] gathered. . . .' But
winter brought disaster.

Regrettably, there is no certainty as to the shape of the
disaster. Some accounts mention rumours of Indian attack;
others speak of leadership conflict between Gilbert and the
elderly and indecisive George Popham. In any case, a supply ship arriving in the spring of 1608—after a winter
called, by the same contemporary account, 'unseasonable'
and 'vehement'—found that George Popham and several
other colonists had died and that an unexplained fire had
wiped out the storehouse and much of the provisions. The
same ship brought news that Gilbert's brother Sir John
had died in England, leaving him a goodly inheritance;
Gilbert naturally made ready to go home. Thus robbed of
leaders, and perhaps not anxious to face any more New
England winters, the other colonists went with him—and
the settlement was abandoned.

The Plymouth Company had at least underlined the
English presence on that coast which Gosnold's abortive
colony had first asserted. But afterwards much of the money
(mainly Southampton's) of that company was diverted into
the activities of the London or Virginia Company, whose
Jamestown enterprise had not been abandoned. New
England went back to being a place visited by explorers,
not by settlers: Henry Hudson, for one, sailed its coastal
waters in 1609; more Frenchmen came and looked interest-
edly at the region in ensuing years. Some, indeed, led by
Jesuit missionaries, set up an embryonic colony in Maine

7

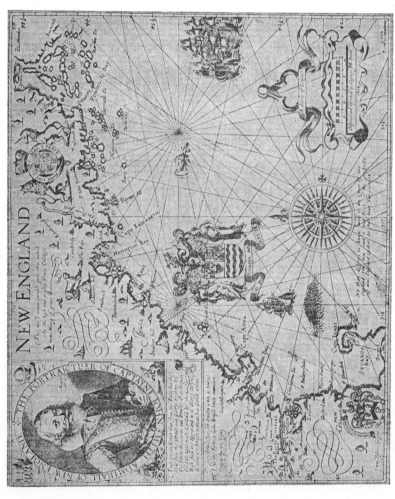

Captain John Smith's map of New England, 1614, with a portrait of Smith in the upper left-hand corner

in 1613, but were forcefully expelled from there by Sir Samuel Argall, a tough English sea-captain sailing from Virginia in a well-armed ship. Then, shortly after this one Virginian had kept New England English, another Virginian came along to lead the still unsettled land into a new era.

John Smith, whose name exists in historical myth as the beloved of Pocahontas, was in historical fact a strong leader of men who had kept Jamestown colony intact during its difficult early years, until illness led to a loosening of his grip, and his return to England in 1610. In 1614 he decided to occupy himself with New England on his country's behalf. With two ships he arrived at Monhegan Island, northwards from the mouth of the Kennebec, then cast about back and forth along the coast, examining the land with an eye well versed in the needs of colonies, while his men loaded a saleable cargo of fish, and some furs. With this cargo, which realized about £1,500, he returned to England and wrote an immensely valuable account of his explorations, including a remarkably accurate and detailed map of the area.

The account let the English in on the secret of how immense America is, and exactly what odds and obstacles confronted the maker of minute colonies on its less hospitable edges. In his more detailed passages Smith wrote, as had others before him, of New England's splendid harbours, the superabundant fish, the vast stands of good timber in the wilds, the quantity of game and the dense population in some areas of Indians. He also traced his path in fairly fine specifics, describing all the places he touched on— Cape Cod's 'excellent harbour', the navigable Penobscot river, the fertile banks of the Kennebec and more. But unlike so many of his predecessors he turned his back on the attractions of Maine. In one of the most striking parts of his discourse, he announces that Massachusetts, instead, 'is the paradise of all those parts'. And on that subject he waxed fairly eloquent:

> Who can but approve this a most excellent place, both for health and fertility? And of all the four parts of the world that I have yet seen not inhabited, could I have but means to transport a colony, I would rather live here than anywhere: and if it did not maintain

itself, were we but once indifferently well fitted, let us starve.

Strong feelings from the former Virginian. Or, at any rate, strong propaganda. And he continued:

> Here are no hard landlords to rack us with high rents, or extorted fines to consume us; no tedious pleas in law to consume us with their many years disputations for justice.... Here every man may be master and owner of his own labour and land.... If he have nothing but his hands, he may set up his trade, and by industry quickly grow rich....

These sentiments, of course, are the standard appeals to the 'huddled masses yearning to breathe free' found throughout the history of emigration. Smith was the first, and most listened to, user of this appeal on New England's behalf.

But he is (or should be) remembered by New Englanders for even more concrete reasons. He named the place: his account was entitled *A Description of New England*, and the name stuck. He had mapped the place, too, from which future navigators would profit; and he had broadcast to his nation the fact that profit (as well as 'paradise') was to be found there. Smith himself never profited from his achievement beyond that initial £1,500: on his return he had met Gorges and though the two men shared an enthusiasm for New England neither could afford to realize on it. The Plymouth Company was now virtually defunct, and Gorges' grandiose plans had come to little. A tiny expedition—two ships, sixteen would-be colonists and Smith—was set up to plant a colony in 1615, but a storm shattered the first attempt, and the second attempt collapsed when pirates attacked the ships and held Smith prisoner for some months. A third attempt consisted of three ships and a proposed fifteen-man colony, but costs mounted while the ships lay at anchor awaiting a fair wind, and eventually the merchant backers cut their losses and abandoned the enterprise, so that the anchors never were lifted.

By this time there may have been Englishmen who believed, if they thought about the place at all, that New

England was under a special cloud of ill luck. Certainly John Smith came to be considered something of a Jonah, by Gorges among others, though Gorges' own touch on colonization ventures had always coincided with disaster —indeed, the Plymouth Company gave up plans for colonies after Smith's third failure. But in the face of this discouragement there still existed Smith's glowing—and increasingly widely read—accounts of New England. There can be no doubt that the migrating Puritans of later years went that way partly because some of them recalled how highly and convincingly Smith had praised the place. But before those religious refugees went looking for paradise in Massachusetts, others—also refugees, though somewhat different in their viewpoints—found their way there mostly by accident, and stayed to be the first New Englanders.

# 2. 'They Knew They Were Pilgrims'

In seventeenth-century England, if anyone needs reminding, politics were riddled with religious concerns, religion was a political matter, established church and state were one. Therefore any form of religious dissent and nonconformity was in fact a crime against the state, and people holding such views made themselves vulnerable to much unpleasant official harassment and persecution. Yet there were nonconformists in plenty, willing to risk this often painful disapproval because of their unflinching belief that the English Reformation had not gone far enough towards true Protestantism, that the theological attitudes and forms of worship within the established church still smelled too strongly of 'papist' ways, and needed purifying. So these non-conformists acquired the label 'Puritans', under which was loosely grouped a considerable variety of sects and schismatics, all brandishing their particular doctrinal differences as the only acceptable form of the revealed Truth.

Some of these dissenters remained members of the established church and worked for their 'second reformation' from within. Others stepped away from the church, forming churches of their own, which as a criminal act made them constantly the victims of arrests, fines, imprisonment and so on. In 1607 one such 'separatist' church—in the hamlet of Scrooby, in Nottinghamshire—could live no longer in circumstances of strain and fear. The congregation as a whole decided to emigrate—to Holland, the one nation in Europe that made a point of religious toleration. The religious climate in Holland had tempted other nonconformist English groups before the Scrooby people; their example may have provided some of the encouragement needed by these quiet villagers before they could uproot themselves and cross the Channel. Once they had done so, however, coming to rest in Amsterdam, the slightly differing doctrines held by some of the other English emigrés in that city drove the Scrooby group, after less than a year, to separate themselves even more fully, by moving to a smaller centre in Holland, Leyden.

There the Scrooby congregation settled in and stayed for eleven years. But, for many, these were not comfortable nor especially happy years. The Dutch language made life difficult; and not all of the emigrants found work that was remunerative or congenial. But they might have put up with these lesser hardships, except for the more serious problem that their children, like the children of all emigrants anywhere, were naturally becoming more and more assimilated: they would grow up speaking Dutch, would probably marry Dutch citizens and so on. This threat to the English heritage and the communal closeness of the separatist community worried its leaders—as to some extent did the comparatively free and easy Dutch way of life, offering iniquitous temptation, by Scrooby lights, to the young. The answer clearly was yet another emigration. And, because the problems of assimilation, temptation and/or persecution were likely to arise just about anywhere else in the civilized world, some of the separatists began to speak in favour of starting from scratch in the uncivilized world of America.

These considerations arose in about 1617, when John Smith's propagandizing for the region he called New England was in full spate, and when reports were also coming back of progress in Virginia and continuing voyages of discovery elsewhere in the New World. But naturally the Scrooby exiles could not discuss the idea further without knowing whether such an emigration was economically practicable. Two men went to London to look into the matter—and also to assure any prospective backers or government officials that they were not manic zealots but sober and industrious people.

It took these representatives nearly two years to find the way to America. The existence of Jamestown led them to fix their hopes on Virginia, but the London (Virginia) Company that held the right to settle that region was in some financial difficulty and proved both difficult and dilatory. At that point the group might well have taken up a tentative offer from Holland to settle in the area called New Amsterdam, at the mouth of the Hudson river. But then they came into contact with a London entrepreneur named Thomas Weston, who may have been something of a schemer but who was also a man of action. Weston believed colonies could mean profit, and found other businessmen who believed the same: they formed a joint stock company, while Weston managed somehow to get a 'patent' to make a settlement within the lands of the Virginia Company. Meanwhile, because the Leyden representatives had discretely proffered themselves as sober, loyal and as far removed as possible from religious subversion, James I had issued an undertaking not to molest or harry them providing they remained peaceable.

The would-be emigrants then began to worry about the terms of the arrangement, under which each adult 'planter' (emigrant, colonist) would hold a £10 share, as would each 'merchant adventurer' gathered by Weston. But the company was to hold as common property not only capital, profits and so on but also the houses, improved land, even gardens of the settlers. And all this common property was to be divided among all the shareholders after seven years, which meant that the individual colonist would not after all that time own even his own vegetable garden. These and other more detailed conditions led to considerable acrimony, and many of those separatists who had first planned to join the enterprise now withdrew. Weston and company promptly signed up a group of non-separatist English folk who were willing to try pioneering the New World. The Leyden group then refused to sign the agreement that bore these conditions; Weston responded by cutting off the flow of capital.

And all this was at the eleventh hour—for some time earlier in 1620, the company had chartered a ship of 180 tons called the *Mayflower*, while the Leyden community had added a smaller ship, the *Speedwell*, of 60 tons, which they intended to keep with them in their colony after the larger vessel had deposited them and turned home. With these arrangements made, and with some considerable investment (not least in the cost of making the *Speedwell* more seaworthy than she had been at the time of purchase), it seemed wrong to the Leyden group that the enterprise should be aborted. Surely, they felt, the contractual problems could eventually be overcome along with all the other difficulties of such a complicated plan. So, on the *Speedwell*, about fifty Leyden separatists sailed home to England.

The story of these people and the colony they made was first told—and probably best told—in the clear, rich and strong prose of William Bradford, who became the colonists' most notable leader, in his *History of Plymouth Plantation*. Bradford it was who gave the emigrants their famous name, when he wrote of their saddened departure from Leyden,

> that goodly and pleasant city which had been their resting-place for near 12 years; but they knew they were pilgrims, and looked not much on those things, but lifted up their eyes to the heavens, their dearest country, and quieted their spirits.

Bradford also wrote, concerning the start of the enterprise, 'it was granted the dangers were great, but not desperate; the difficulties were many, but not invincible...'. Few of his group might have shared that optimism during the early years—or indeed during the early days, for dangers and difficulties arose almost at once, even aside from the cut-off flow of financial support. The contractual problems were not solved: the agreement remained unsigned, Weston remained adamant, and the colonists remained determined. In the end they sold much of their badly needed provisions to clear their debts so that they could weigh anchor. When the two ships finally sailed for the New World, with about 120 people (ninety on the *Mayflower*) it was early August, late in the year to begin one of those arduous Atlantic crossings that would become so commonplace in succeeding centuries of emigration. And then the departure was held up again, for the *Speedwell* belied its name, turning out to be dangerously leaky. Back they went to Southampton, to waste two weeks more patching and caulking. At sea again, the smaller ship still proved unseaworthy, the captain announcing that even continuous pumping could barely keep her afloat. Back they went again, this time to Plymouth. And there they abandoned the *Speedwell*, and transferred as many of her passengers as could be accommodated to the *Mayflower*—which meant leaving nearly twenty people behind.

*A seventeenth-century depiction of the farewell to the* Mayflower *as i departed from Plymouth*

## 'They Knew They Were Pilgrims'

After this saddening and dispiriting separation, the *May-flower* sailed bravely away into early September Atlantic weather, taking with her 102 passengers—about forty of them from the separatist community in Holland. Aside from a dozen servants and hired men, the rest were the non-separatist emigrants signed up by Weston (mostly from London, a few from the south-east of England or from around Southampton). Each group contained seventeen men, each had an almost equal number of women and children; each group was made up of ordinary English people, from the same social 'class' in that still strongly hierarchical society. Yet they dwelt upon their distinctions more than their similarities—distinctions as spelt out when the two groups took on the factional labels of 'saints' and 'strangers'. The Leyden saints, who imposed a kind of minority rule, created a good deal of outrage and dissension with the insistence by some of them that their religious practices be followed by the whole company. They also annoyed the seamen, largely by being sanctimonious. At the same time there were those among the strangers who had equally antagonized the Leyden emigrants with their rough intolerance of the separatists' beliefs, and the sailors with their irritating tendency to interfere with the running of the ship.

So it was an edgy crossing, and physical conditions did not improve matters. The weather was generally demanding—which meant cold, rain, heavy seas and gale-force winds. The food was poor, the staples being dried fish, salt meat, said to have been horse, and ship's biscuit. And, during the *sixty-six days* that the crossing required, most of the provisions ran frighteningly short. The passengers were unpleasantly crowded, which meant a degree of insanitariness dangerous and nasty even in seventeenth-century terms. Then, in October, the Atlantic began to live up to its worst reputation—day upon day of frightful storms and gales, so fierce that the ship could carry no sail at all. As always with the old wooden ships, the lashing of tremendous seas caused the seams to work open, and the freezing water drenched the passengers—who were huddled below in the fetid hold because only professionals could survive on the pitching decks. (One passenger, risking all for a breath of air, went on deck and was predictably washed overboard—but was miraculously rescued from the teeth of the storm.) At the height of the storm one of the massive beams amidships cracked and began to give way. The seamen began to mutter about turning back, but the captain ordered the beam braced and assured everyone that the ship could continue.

So continue it did, and as the year turned into November they were only days from their destination. It was then that the only death of the voyage occurred—from one of the common shipboard diseases like 'ship's fever'. To have managed the crossing with only one death was even more miraculous than rescuing a man overboard in a gale: in those days people died like flies on long voyages, as in 1619, when on a ship carrying about 180 colonists to Virginia about 130 were said not to have survived the crossing. Also, one of the women had given birth on the voyage (some accounts say there were two births) which meant that a full complement of Pilgrims were looking longingly over the *Mayflower*'s rail on 10 November at a jut of land that was the shore of Cape Cod.

But that was not where they wanted to be, as they well knew. The lands on which they were intended to settle lay within the domain of the Virginia Company, stretching north no farther than the present boundary of New Jersey. The captain turned the ship south, but the wind was against them and the coast began to present 'dangerous shoals and roaring breakers'. Besides, there were those on board who felt they could not survive another moment on the heaving decks. So the captain turned about again, swung round the point of Cape Cod, and anchored in the capacious harbour where Provincetown now stands.

At that point these devout people gave thanks to God, as they were to do at fairly frequent intervals in the next few calamitous months. The thanks, rather than the calamities, seem to have lived on in American historical legend—where the impression seems to be given that after rising from their thanksgiving prayers the Pilgrims had very little more to worry about. Instead, from our point of view, they had very little to give thanks for—and would have less and less as time went on. As they stood, at Provincetown, though only one had died, nearly all the ship's company were seriously weakened from lack of adequate food: some had the beginnings of scurvy, while the drenchings of the stormy crossing had left many also beginning to suffer from bronchial and allied complaints. They could hardly have been in a worse state to face their first New England winter, with its promise of continuing hunger, inadequate shelter and unremitting labour. Indeed, four of the company died during the few weeks when the *Mayflower* was at Provincetown. One of the dead was Bradford's wife Dorothy: we are told she died of drowning, but there seems more than a hint that her death was self-inflicted. (She had had to leave behind her five-year-old child, when the *Speedwell* had been abandoned, which no doubt deepened her misery.) If she did kill herself—in spite of the horror with which suicide would be viewed by someone of her religious beliefs—Dorothy Bradford's death gives an idea of just how grim the Pilgrims found the prospect before them.

Winter was moving rapidly into the 'hideous and desolate wilderness', as Bradford saw their surroundings; it was of extreme urgency that a place be found to settle, to build some form of houses, before too long. An armed and armoured group of men went on shore to explore, led by Captain Miles Standish—a diminutive but oak-tough professional soldier whose prominent place in the Pilgrim legend comes from an instance of having acted as matchmaker, but who was in fact hired, as one of the strangers, to take charge of the protection and defence of the colony. As they stumbled through the rough and heavily forested country, watching carefully for signs of Indians, friendly or otherwise, they came upon some man-made mounds in the vicinity. Some proved to be Indian burials, which Standish properly refused to disturb further. But others held stores of Indian corn—maize. The Pilgrims, in days to come, dug up a good few bushels of the corn, salving their conscience by agreeing that the Indians, once met, would be repaid. In this way they satisfied one desperate need—for seed with which to begin planting in spring against the *next* winter's hunger.

But as for this winter, the Pilgrims reluctantly concluded that Provincetown ought not be their new home. The bay was not all that satisfactory: ships had to stand too far out from shore. And there was no adequate supply of fresh water to the seaside sites available for building. So more explorers went farther abroad, including one group who took the shallop, an open boat that could be sailed or rowed, to a bay that had the name of Thievish Harbour—

perhaps aptly, for these borrowers of other people's corn. It proved to be a well-sheltered anchorage, and to have satisfactory soil on shore (Indian cornfields were plentiful) as well as a number of clear streams. When this group had reported back, the Pilgrims gratefully accepted this new providence, and the captain of the *Mayflower* swung his ship south-westward and anchored no more than a mile from shore in the harbour that soon shed its embarrassing older name, given by some passing fishermen, and acquired permanently the name John Smith had given it: Plymouth Bay.

There further thanks were given and the Plymouth Rock received its immortality. But by then it was mid-December, and there was no longer any time before full winter struck with all its ferocity. Storms fell upon the group in crude temporary shelters on land—wind and freezing rain and snow, so that their work was constantly interrupted by the weather. But slowly the site of New Plymouth began to resemble a colony. From the beach the men laid out a straight street, climbing to the foot of a hill; along the street building lots were marked out, while Standish and his men quickly erected a temporary platform on the hill to support protective cannon. At the beach end of the street, the individual householders and their families laboriously began to put up the cottages so badly needed. All these structures were built in the plain English way of wattle-and-daub—or as close an approximation as could be managed with pioneer American materials—with their steep roofs carefully thatched.

The thatching betrayed them, in the freezing depths of January, when the roof of the completed Common House caught fire. Some priceless stores were destroyed in the blaze, but no one was hurt. It was just as well—for the winter and lack of shelter had been taking a sufficiently terrible toll of the meagre population. Six died in December, eight in January, seventeen in February—it was called a 'general sickness', though undoubtedly some succumbed from scurvy, some from pneumonic complications, some possibly from sheer exposure and overwork. By late March, when all of the exhausted Pilgrims were finally able to move into their new cottages, *half* the company had died —not to mention about half the crew of the *Mayflower*. At one point only about six people were strong enough to be on their feet—yet risking their own collapse by pains-takingly caring for the sick and dying.

In the face of this catastrophic winter, and considering the potential for the saints *versus* strangers conflict that had emerged during the voyage, it remains astonishing that the community held together so well as a co-operative and organized unit. To some extent, the string of disasters helped, for common disaster can be a great unifier. But it might not have done so without the strength of character of the community leaders—John Carver, who had been chosen governor, sturdy Miles Standish, William Bradford. And this leadership could be exercised so successfully be-cause the Pilgrims had, while at Provincetown, chosen to impose upon themselves a remarkable form of political authority, the famous 'Mayflower Compact'.

The need for this authority came out of intimations of anarchy voiced by some of the strangers, off the shores of New England. These rebellious individuals pointed out that the Pilgrims were not landing in Virginia, for which their patent intended them—and so neither patent nor any other source of authority existed in the New England wilderness. They began to announce that they would 'use their own liberty, since none had power to command them' once they were ashore. The Leyden saints had to act quickly to crush this destructive mood before it could be translated into action. So they and the steadier element among the strangers formulated a document, in some ways resembling one of the religious 'covenants' so favoured in separatist churches.

Forty-one adult men came together to sign the Compact, terming themselves a 'civil body politic' and pledging them-selves

> to enact, constitute and frame such just and equal laws, ordinances, acts, constitutions and offices, from time to time, as shall be thought most meet and convenient for the general good of the Colony, unto which we prom-ise all due submission and obedience.

Political scientists have licked their lips ever since over this praiseworthy move by the tiny colony away from the standard European ideas of government current in their time. Needless to say, the Compact did not mean that

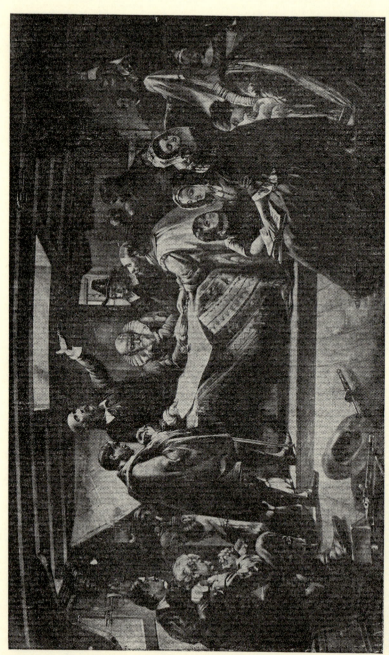

The signing of the Mayflower Compact, after Edwin White's, standing by the table on the left. Will a Standish seated at

colonial America had taken one giant step into full and outright egalitarian democracy. The signatories of the Compact were the adult male householders: women, servants and other second-class citizens did not get a look in. But, if not fully democratic, the Compact was undoubtedly a legitimate 'social contract' in which civil authority was vested in the will of the *majority* of the adult men—not in that of the privileged few of noble birth. In the seventeenth century such a 'body politic' was quite revolutionary enough.

At the time of the Compact the Pilgrims also performed the second major exercise of their communal will, in choosing—by popular (adult male) election, another near-democratic technique by which the separatist communities had long selected their pastors—John Carver as the colony's first governor. During the first winter Carver had to bring his authority as chief executive to bear on a few new stirrings of unrest and disobedience. But the majority remained concerned for 'the general good of the colony' and soon the mutterings of discontent were silenced and that remarkable communality restored.

Its restoration was no doubt aided by a general and increasing nervousness among the Pilgrims in the face of a potential common danger—from the human inhabitants of the wilderness. From the day of their arrival the colonists had seen signs of the presence of Indians—the cleared fields, a few abandoned huts found by Standish in the forest. During the winter, smoke from Indian fires was occasionally spotted, and occasionally a colonist working outside the village might see a few human forms slipping through the underbrush. But aside from these sightings, there had been nothing. And the less the Pilgrims saw of Indians, the more nervous they became.

Standish, whose position as commander of the armed men among the company had been confirmed by another due process of election, insisted that muskets and blunderbusses be kept in as good condition as weather permitted. And it may have been partly this visible readiness, along with some noisily impressive trial firings of the cannon on the hill, that forestalled early contacts with the Indians. But there was another reason for the absence of the Indians from that region. The colonists learned about it one astonishing day in March, when the first signs of spring had brought a general brightening of their mood. On that day an armed, painted and nearly naked Indian walked calmly into the village and spoke to the Pilgrims in English.

His name was Samoset, and he was a visitor to Plymouth, coming from a tribe in Maine, where he had learned his sparse English through trading with British seamen and fishermen. He told them that the principal chief of assorted small and loosely allied tribes around Plymouth was named Massasoit, whose base of operations was near Narragansett. And, most importantly, he told the Pilgrims that normally the site of New Plymouth was the home of a fierce tribe called the Patuxet, who with other tribes had been nearly wiped out in 1617 by an epidemic of smallpox, undoubtedly an infection from white traders. Here was the tragic reason for the scarcity of Indians in the bay region—which the Pilgrims tended to see as another instance of Providence going on before to ease the way for them.

After considerable socializing, Samoset left—and within a few days returned to herald the approach of Massasoit himself and sixty of his tall braves. This historic meeting involved all the usual speech-making, gift-giving, feasting —and a certain amount of suspicion on both sides, clearing only slowly—that usually marked the non-violent first contacts between Indians and Europeans. Of almost equal importance, though, were two other results of this meeting and the friendliness that grew up between the two communities. The Pilgrims had seen in the Indians' willingness to trade beaver skins a future source of badly needed income; and Massasoit had brought with him a Patuxet Indian whose name, Tisquantum, the Pilgrims pronounced Squanto, who spoke much better English than Samoset. Squanto had been carried off to England by an English sea-captain six years before, and had jumped ship on a return voyage. He acted as interpreter during the crucial meeting with Massasoit, and he stayed with the Pilgrims afterwards—as instructor, friend, 'special instrument sent of God'.

It was Squanto, then, when spring finally managed to free the earth for planting, who passed on to the Pilgrims those skills and that local knowledge without which they would certainly have perished. He showed them how to make hillocks in which to plant the seed corn they had stolen from Provincetown, and how to fertilize the corn with fish, and warned them to guard the fields every moment against birds and other corn-eating creatures. He guided them on hunting expeditions, teaching them much about the game and the ways of the wilderness. And he aided them in their frequent contacts with Massasoit's Indians, whether social or commercial—but more increasingly the latter, now, as the Pilgrims stored up beaver skins for sale in Europe.

All this organized and productive activity, along with the rapidly improving health of the colonists, no doubt eased some of the misgivings and sadness felt when the *Mayflower* weighed anchor in April to return to England. She went without a cargo, which upset the colony's financial backers, and with only half a crew—but without even one colonist making the return voyage. Disgruntled, dispirited, weak from illness and half-starved the Pilgrims still might have been—yet all of the survivors of that winter felt, rightly, that matters could only improve, and were happy to set about creating that improvement.

April, too, brought the death of John Carver, perhaps from overwork in the fields after the illness and privations of the winter. William Bradford was elected governor in his place, and was able to preside over a splendid first summer. Abundant game and fish had supplemented the meagre rations that remained from the stores brought on the *Mayflower*; the Indian corn sprouted so well that about a peck per week, some eight to ten pounds, of maize could be allocated to each colonist. Work progressed on the settlement, so that eleven sound houses now stood along the first street. And the local Indians had become their friends and helpers. All these benefits came to the Pilgrims' mind, no doubt, during that autumnal harvest feast (Massasoit attended it with ninety braves, but brought more than enough game to the tables to compensate) which is now commemorated in America's ritual Thanksgiving meal.

But not so long after the celebration, as autumn deepened, the Pilgrims' hearts must have sunk again. In the offing was another fearsome winter—and though the strengthening summer might help to hold off another epidemic, the colonists had still not been able to store up food enough to feel secure during the dark months when weather inhibited hunting and the fish left the Plymouth shores.

They probably would have spent the winter half-starved anyway: but in November rations had to be shortened distressingly further when a ship named the *Fortune* sailed into the bay, bearing thirty-five more would-be colonists—and carrying not one ounce of supplies.

The *Fortune* had been dispatched by Weston and his 'merchant adventurers', and aside from the passengers carried a letter from Weston complaining of the *Mayflower*'s lack of cargo. It also insisted that the Pilgrims sign the agreement that they had rejected before sailing: there was a visible if unstated connection between this insistence and the lack of supplies, and so with reluctance the Pilgrims signed. As one bright spot, Weston had managed to secure a patent for the colony from the still extant, if inactive, Plymouth Company—so the Pilgrims' position in New England was now more or less legalized. But with thirty-five more mouths to feed, legality was the least of their worries.

As for these newcomers, only about twelve were further arrivals from the Leyden community of separatists. The others had been recruited by Weston in England, mainly from London—and mostly single young men, 'many of them wild enough', as Bradford regretfully put it. But at least the extra hands were reasonably welcome, for as always an immense amount of work had to be done. The *Fortune* was loaded with £500 worth of beaver pelts and cedar wood, and sent home; and no doubt Weston would have been delighted, and some of the colony's supply problems solved, if the ship had lived up to its name. But it was attacked and stripped of the cargo by French pirates, and the Pilgrims' labours went for nothing.

News of this calamity would not reach the colony for months, of course, but by then the colony already had calamities enough. Massasoit and his unpredictable Indians slowly came to the conclusion that Squanto, through his well-armed white friends, had acquired too much power. They demanded that Squanto be turned out of the colony, and handed over to them—obviously, to be killed. While Bradford delayed, Standish busied his men building a stockade of upright logs round the whole village, and starting work on a secure fort on the hill to replace the gun platform. In the face of these preparations, Massasoit's threats came to nothing; but then there came another sort of invasion. A boat landed in the bay, from a ship sent over by Weston (as a separate venture) to fish, cut timber and gather salt. In a letter brought to the colony by the seven men on the boat, Weston asked the Pilgrims to feed and shelter these men while they worked on land; and at the same time he informed them crushingly that low finances meant there was no chance that further Leyden emigrants could be sent over.

Thus swollen further, the little community struggled as best it could through the winter, aided by contributions from English vessels fishing off Maine which had been solicited by one of the Winslows, a leading Pilgrim family. Even so, each person was on less than half rations for months—a vicious circle, for it weakened them so they were less able to hunt and fish (when the fish returned), and less able to work competently in the fields when spring returned. And of course the arduous work of fort-building went on still: the edifice took ten months to complete. In June two more ships came from England, sent by Weston. The company backing New Plymouth was coming apart, according to the news these ships brought; but Weston had obtained a patent for another colonial venture, and these ships carried sixty people, none of them a separatist, to populate this new colony. Yet Weston had the temerity to request that the starving Pilgrims feed and shelter these newcomers until the ships completed a voyage south to Virginia and back. And of course the charitable Pilgrims did so, even though the sixty new colonists lent scarcely a hand in the building and the tilling, and in fact extensively pilfered the Pilgrims' corn as it ripened.

With the extra mouths, the stealing and the under-nourished Pilgrim farmers' physical weakness, the harvest was desperately poor that autumn—and the most devout concern for Christian charity did not prevent the Pilgrims from feeling some relief when the sixty newcomers finally sailed off to set up their colony at Wessagusset (now Weymouth in Massachusetts), twenty-five miles from New Plymouth. The Pilgrim leaders turned anxiously to trading with the Indians for the corn they needed to survive that winter; meanwhile the autumn itself brought one notable death, that of Squanto, struck down by some white man's illness but still hoping for a place in the white man's heaven.

Squanto's demise, and the Pilgrims' assistance in helping Massasoit back to health when he became seriously ill, repaired relations somewhat with the local Indians. Over at Wessagusset, though, the relations had gone badly awry. Those colonists, rough and ready men for the most part, had badly antagonized the Indians by cheating them, taking their women, finally by turning beggar—which the Indians despised—when their own supplies ran out. Massasoit warned New Plymouth that the Wessagusset colony was to be attacked, and that the Indians would probably attack the Pilgrims as well. Fiery Miles Standish, never willing to let an enemy fire the first shot, took some men to warn the other whites, and then addressed himself to the local Indians—taking it upon himself not only to punish the ringleaders of the proposed rising (some were hanged) but also to kill the main leader personally, in hand-to-hand combat. The distressed colonists of Wessagusset gathered up what belongings they had left and fled to Maine, hoping to pick up passage to England. And though Standish and the Pilgrims were sharply criticized over this bloody handling of the situation, from historians later as well as from some of their spiritual mentors back in Leyden, the colonists could at least point out that they had no further trouble from the local Indian tribes.

With these alarms and violences the colony came once again through a miserable winter of near-famine and some fright. In the spring of 1623, trying to rationalize their unreliable agriculture, the Pilgrims abandoned the communal tillage they had begun with and allocated plots of land, about an acre each, to individual households—with prearranged contributions from these to supply the fishermen or the defenders who had less time to work in fields. An early drought damaged their hopes briefly, but the fish returned as plentiful as ever and the rain finally fell. That spring also brought new faces to the shores of the region—some because the quiescent Plymouth Company, and Sir Ferdinando Gorges, had stirred again into action.

Gorges and Company had managed in 1620 to wheedle out of the king the formation of a new organization called the 'Council ... for the Planting, Ruling, and Governing of New England'. The Council, replacing the Company, now held proprietory and settlement rights over all land from 40° to 48°—which, in coastal terms, means from New

Jersey north to New Brunswick. (Needless to say, the French and Dutch residents within this span of land were not consulted.) A small and sporadic flow of settlers began to follow—as when a number of men from Devon's Plymouth planted tiny settlements in Rye, New Hampshire, on Monhegan Island and elsewhere. None of these even approximated the size of New Plymouth—nor did the colony established (on the Wessagusset site vacated earlier) by Gorges' son, Captain Robert. He unnerved the Pilgrims briefly, when he arrived in the autumn of 1623, by announcing that he was officially, by royal charter, the governor of *all* New England—as the Council's local representative. But Gorges did not take well to the onset of a typical New England winter, and soon took himself back to England—whereupon his colonists lost heart, and either straggled home themselves or drifted down to Virginia. So, while the occasional tiny settlement remained here and there along the coast—seldom more than a handful of men each, eking out their living by fishing and trading with the Indians—the Pilgrim colony remained the largest and most populous settlement in the region.

And it became still more populous in 1623, when two shiploads more of Leyden saints and London strangers had found the means to emigrate to New Plymouth. The ships held eighty-seven new colonists—twenty-nine of them from Leyden, which meant many long and emotional reunions made even more moving by the newcomers' foreboding sight of the ragged, thin and weary colonists. But for once the soil proved bountiful that year—perhaps because the new system of private-enterprise tillage spurred the Pilgrims to greater efforts. The bumper crop brought a surplus of corn to New Plymouth, and for the first time the colonists could anticipate a winter when they would not be on the edge of famine.

One of the emigrant ships then returned to London, bearing furs and timber and also bearing Edward Winslow who was to buy necessities for the colony. No pirates impeded this progress, and in spring 1624 Winslow returned with a few badly needed cattle, some equipment for fishing and drying and salting the catch—and a minister. But he was not a separatist, soon antagonized the saints with his Anglican ways, and then began plotting with some restless spirits among the newly arrived strangers to take over and alter the colony's religious and legislative basis. The Pilgrims discovered the plot and expelled the minister and his friends. But even with the departure of trouble-makers, and the abundance of food, there continued to be no shortage of trouble. The company formed by Weston that had backed the colony was now almost completely split up, and supplies that arrived in 1625 had in fact to be bought directly by the hard-up Pilgrims, at extortionate prices. Of two shiploads of fish, furs and so on sent back to England, one was taken by pirates and the other found that in the strife and unrest flaming throughout England the bottom had fallen out of the market.

Still, the Pilgrims scrimped and saved and laboured heroically. And, when the final break-up occurred of Weston's original company, they found a way to pay off some debts and acquire title to their own colony. They agreed to buy out the remaining backers for a sum of £1,800 (though the figures indicate that the company had by then sunk about £7,000 into the venture) to be paid off in annual £200 instalments. It would put a frightful strain on the limited earning power of the 180 colonists—but they knew they would manage it, because if they did they would own New Plymouth and everything in it.

By 1627 all these matters had been settled, and the colonists had managed to divide the property that was now theirs fairly among themselves—freehold ownership of houses, a cow and a few pigs for every six people, house-holders to share the burden of paying off the colony's remaining debts, largely through fur trading, and so on. Without any question, the colony had finally gained its feet, even if it could be seen now and then, financially speaking, to stagger a trifle. As the late 1620s continued the Pilgrims expanded the Indian trade, profiting from the growing European interest in North American furs, and traded successfully also with the new Dutch settlements, in what is now New York, and with the fishing fleets.

Clearly all that these thrifty and hard-working folk had needed was the impetus of one or two good years, without too many extraordinary hardships or problems. Not that they were quite free of such troubles yet. Several tiny nuclei of Englishmen, as mentioned before, continued to exist along the New England coast. Most of these 'strag-gling planters', as Bradford called them, lived in harmony with Plymouth and indeed depended upon it for support in their own times of need. But one such nucleus, formed in 1625 on Massachusetts Bay and usually given the apt name of 'Merry Mount', had gathered to it a number of rowdies whose behaviour was compared by the scandalized Bradford to those of 'mad Bacchanalians'—especially when they had erected a maypole to preside over their drunken feasts and pursuits of Indian women. Eventually these lively colonists began selling liquor and guns to the Indians, which terrified the other 'straggling planters'. They asked New Plymouth for help; it was readily given. Miles Standish marched out with his men, laid siege to the offending colony, and farcically found its residents too drunk to fight. The leaders were imprisoned until they could be sent back to England, and the others expelled from New England.

Also in the late 1620s further departures from Leyden managed to bring to Plymouth almost all the remaining Leyden saints. They came in two groups, one in 1629 and one in 1630—and though other individuals and families from Holland would make their own way to Plymouth in succeeding years, the Leyden emigration was now virtually complete. To add to the sense of completion, a new patent had been drawn up (by the Council for New England) for the colony, stipulating more clearly where the boundaries of New Plymouth lay—and also stipulating the colony's control, for trading purposes, of land on the Kennebec river in Maine.

So there was New Plymouth in 1630—its first pioneers united with their loved ones from Holland, wavering on the edge of prosperity, seemingly secure in ownership of its land and domination, commercial and military, of more land around it. Yet slightly to the north that year there was beginning an emigration that was eventually to undermine that security, conclude that domination and in the end swallow up that independence. The English Puritans were landing in Massachusetts.

# 3. The Puritan Flight

In those years when the Pilgrims were growing accustomed to the taste of wild turkey and Indian corn, and building towards something resembling peace and prosperity in the tiny coastal scratch they had made on the face of America's wilderness immensity, momentous developments in England had thoroughly undermined any old world peace and prosperity. The dour but decisive James I had gone to his grave, leaving behind him a country sorely distressed by inflation, by political disorder and by religious unrest. It was a country, in short, being badly shaken by living through a violent time of transition, which its leaders, as hindsight conveniently tells us, generally failed wholly to comprehend.

Charles I especially failed to comprehend most of the problems and necessities of national leadership. Faced with a Parliament that, however undemocratic it was, had begun to find itself as a political power, Charles tried to force its compliance to his ideas for extracting money from the nobility, then petulantly dissolved it in 1629—an approach almost calculated to create subversion. The climate of unrest was not improved by the disastrous near-collapse of the cloth industry in the late 1620s, which threw thousands out of work and onto the poor-relief rolls of the parishes. More rebellious mutterings could be heard when, in the face of disastrous military failures in Europe, Charles brought his armies home to swell the already intolerable numbers of unemployed—and then billeted these war-brutalized men on England's householders. And, to make matters worse, because he was married to a Catholic queen, he relaxed many of his predecessors' rulings against Catholicism—and in the process strengthened his intolerance towards those non-conformists within the Church of England who objected to the relaxation.

This far from homogeneous group thus suffered perhaps more than others, not only from harassment but also because it included a great many fairly well-off people from the social stratum of 'gentleman' down to that of 'artisan', and this whole range felt especially painfully the impact of the economic cutbacks, the diminution of real income, the dumping of demobbed troops and so on. But unkindest of all cuts was the position their religion put them in— which is why this group, the English Puritans, formed by far the greater part of the mass departures from England to America that were about to begin.

The fact that the Puritans were far from homogeneous is a point worth stressing, if only to counteract the stereo- typed image of them outlined by the modern American historian William H. Goetzmann, as 'a rather dull person in a high-crowned hat, carrying a blunderbuss and a dead turkey'. To the adjective 'dull' recent generations might add 'censorious', since the word *puritanical* has taken on the special meaning of an anti-permissiveness in moral attitudes especially pertaining to sex. But of course the Puritan was not simply a prudish pioneer with fanatical tendencies. He was a man who, in the seventeenth century, held firmly and seriously certain views about forms of re- ligious worship, the nature of religious institutions, and the relations between these and secular institutions—views which did not accord with those put forward by the Estab- lished Church of Britain.

It has been noted earlier that both the separatists who became Pilgrims and the non-conformists who remained within the church were all religious dissenters together, and all could and would be later dubbed Puritans—no matter how differently they exercised their 'pure' dissent. Space does not permit anything like a full account of the dense complexes of thought that distinguished all the various 'isms' within the non-conformist spectrum, whether Plymouth Pilgrims or Massachusetts Puritans or whoever. Still, a few notable and relevant features of Puritanism can be isolated in general; they will not be wholly un- familiar. Most authorities make much play of the basic Puritan concept of man's original sin, and the Calvinist view that we are all 'predestined' to eternal punishment except for a few of the 'elect' who are equally predestined to be saved. Most Puritans considered themselves probably among the elect, and comported themselves accordingly—within a rigidly restrictive moral code, and not without a certain tangible self-satisfaction. As for that moral code, and the social and political corollaries to it, all such matters were unswervingly rooted in God's will. As Protestants, of course, the Puritans fundamentally believed that that will could be perceptible by the individual; but any hint of individuality within the creed stopped there.

So did any hint of tolerance: the Puritans were not fighting for religious *freedom* when they opposed the autocracy (or theocracy) of the established church; they were fighting for the right to *replace* that theocracy with one of their own. Nathaniel Ward, a Puritan apologist, made this point unabashedly explicit:

> He that is willing to tolerate any religion, or discrepant way of religion, beside his own ... either doubts of his own, or is not sincere in it.

And if such grim warning were not enough, another Puritan tract asserted:

> If the devil might have his free option I believe he would ask nothing else but liberty to enfranchise all other religions, and to embondage the true. . . .

As it seemed in the 1620s that the 'true' Puritan way was not improving its position in England, it was transplanted to America where it could hopefully grow without hindrance—and without hindrance could impose its dogmatic, intolerant regimentation.

In Puritan communities the individual's needs were subsumed in the group's, and secular authority became one with religious authority to impose total, unbending orthodoxy of belief and behaviour upon every member. Deviation was quickly and harshly punished—expulsion was among the milder forms, as will be seen. And, to repeat, the orthodoxy was not intended to be manifest only within the church, but to appear in a man's family relations (authoritarian, unbending), business dealings (hardworking, thrifty), recreations (limited, tending to be more useful than pleasurable).

## The Puritan Flight

One might go on, but this general sketch will suffice until it can be filled out by noting the Massachusetts Puritans in action. Certainly it should be clear that men with such beliefs could only have been unhappy in early seventeenth-century England—and not merely because they stood in theological opposition to the Church of England, or because they were oppressed by Charles's increased favouring of Catholicism. Their moral codes were offended by the licentiousness of the 'Carolinian' age; their work ethic was undermined by the economic depression. Such a state of mind was the richest growing ground for thoughts about emigration, especially as the news came back about the immensity of America and the potential there that was barely being tapped by the Virginia colonists or the Pilgrims in New England.

Some of those thoughts took root in the lively mind of a Suffolk squire named John Winthrop, who had watched the real value of his income dwindle with inflation, and who watched his king moving in a direction that would, Winthrop felt, prove dangerous for Puritans. 'I am verily persuaded', he wrote in 1629, 'God will bring some heavy affliction upon this land.' He looked around and saw 'a height of intemperance in excess of riot', 'the fountains of learning and religion . . . corrupted' and in every way he concluded that 'this land grows weary of her inhabitants'. Why, he asked, 'should we stand striving here for places of habitation . . . and in the meantime suffer whole countries as profitable for the use of man to lie waste without any improvement?'

So Puritans were to emigrate to a land where there was space, profitability and the need for improvement. And they aimed themselves, from the outset, at New England—not because of the Pilgrims but because another toehold, as it were, had been made, by men of a like persuasion, some of whom were known within English Puritan circles. This toehold was more important to the Puritan choice of New England than was the Pilgrim presence, for the Pilgrims evinced minutely different shades of religious belief and were therefore viewed with some distaste and animosity. Nonetheless, the forerunners in whom Winthrop became interested had planted themselves on a part of Massachusetts remarkably close to New Plymouth.

These arrivals had set out as a commercial venture backed

35

by a group of West Country merchants mostly in Dorchester. Cape Ann had been chosen for their settlement, and there in 1623 some fourteen men had landed, to seek their profits from fishing. Some complications arose, since Cape Ann was properly within the Plymouth patent, but apparently the Pilgrims worked out a sort of reciprocal arrangement with these fishermen. By 1626, though, the Dorchester group had had insufficient return on their investment, and abandoned the project. One of the Cape Ann men, Roger Conant, who had lived briefly at Plymouth, decided to stay on as a settler in New England; but he left the exposed Cape and made his home within Massachusetts Bay in a comfortable harbour to which he gave the name of Salem.

The continuing presence of Conant, a godly man, seems then to have become something of a magnet for further Puritan thinking about New England emigration. But henceforward a certain complexity of business arrangements began to emerge. Remember that there existed the Council for New England, to which James I had given title to the land between 40° and 48°, and from which the Pilgrims' backers had had to obtain a patent. The Council unfortunately developed a tendency to be somewhat too openhanded: it also gave out a patent to Robert Gorges for the whole of Massachusetts Bay, which took in the Pilgrim colony; and gave out another to the Dorchester group for Cape Ann, which overlapped with the Robert Gorges grant.

Now, to complicate things further, in 1628 a group of Puritan businessmen came together to form the Massachusetts Bay Company, which readily obtained yet another patent from the Council, though Sir Ferdinando Gorges, still dominating the Council, required that the Bay Company do nothing potentially harmful to his son's colonial interests. The Bay Company, with their Puritan interests made expressly clear, sent out one John Endicott or Endecott to take charge of their budding colony—at Salem. He was, in fact, going to prepare a place for his fellows; he took sixty men and some cattle, and made his presence felt early on, by visiting the rumbustious colony at Merry Mount (some time before the Pilgrims cleared it out by force of arms) where he personally hewed down the maypole and issued warnings to the sinful residents.

Endecott's chill and fanatical Puritan ways managed at

the same time to incur a measure of antagonism from
Roger Conant on the one hand and the New Plymouth
Pilgrims on the other; but there were no attempts to dis-
place or even undermine him. By 1629 this advance guard
had settled itself and had reported favourably about the
prospects in New England for English Puritans: Francis
Higginson, a minister, found a few 'discommodities' in
the place, among them 'little flies called mosquitoes', 'sharp
biting frosts' and 'snakes and serpents of strange colours
and huge greatness'. But he also found 'fat black earth',
and fish so abundant that his comrades 'ordinarily take
more than they are able to haul to land'. In all, he concluded,

> Here wants as it were good company of honest Christ-
> ians to bring with them horses, kine and sheep to make
> use of this fruitful land. . . .

In England, the Bay Company had reinforced their
position by seeking royal favour, through a few powerful
noblemen with Puritan leanings, and in 1629 this private
company had obtained a royal *charter*, worth far more than
any patent. It constituted them not only as a trading company with 'proprietary' rights, but as a colonizing corporation under the direction of an elected governor (like a
managing director) and a General Court which would
frame the laws and regulations of the company, and of the
colony. The value of the charter lay especially in the fact
that it gave the company the right of *government* over any
colony established, and that it could be rescinded only by
the Crown, not by the Council for New England or any other
body. Skilfully, the members managed to exclude from the
charter the stipulation that the officers of the company
should be resident in England, as was usually the case with
such colonizing enterprises. By doing so, they laid the
groundwork for their 'company directors' to be colonists
too, exercising control over the colony on the spot—which
would put them a long way away from the Crown's executive power, and would make the colony to all intents and
purposes a *self-governing* entity.

Also in 1629 the company sent out a small fleet of ships
carrying about 350 more pairs of willing pioneer hands,
along with four ministers and considerable livestock. The

Puritans were clearly not going to emigrate without adequate preparation; and, unlike the Pilgrims, they could well afford it. There were involved in the Bay Company members of the lesser aristocracy like Sir Richard Saltonstall and others connected with even greater families like that of the Earl of Lincoln or the Earl of Warwick, aside from many representatives of the fairly substantial landed gentry —like John Winthrop. By then, because of his growing interest in emigration and a new-found talent for organization, Winthrop had found his way not only into the company but into its high-level discussions. So he participated in the flurry of policy decisions that were being made in those busy days. They decided, for instance, on land tenure—200 acres for every £50 invested by company shareholders, more if the shareholder emigrated, fifty acres for each emigrant who did not hold shares. They decided on how much contact should be made with the Indians for purposes of trade and conversion, and intended to avoid any familiarity with the tribes. And they predictably made a number of, to them, vitally important religious decisions —because, after all, by emigrating they were becoming separatists, at least in terms of physical separation from the Church of England, and so could go their own theological or ecclesiastical way. Endecott and his people had already abandoned some of the Anglican ways which they found distasteful, and had already expelled the brothers Browne who objected to this move.

But the most far-reaching decision came when the company chose to take advantage of its charter and transfer its government, or management, to New England—well out of immediate reach of the imposition of any anti-Puritan authority in England. Therefore the first governor of the company, Matthew Craddock, who had not planned to emigrate, stood down in favour of an emigrant governor— and the one elected to the job was the new boy, John Winthrop. He now took firm hold of the immediate problem—to raise and finance a fleet (the £5,000 for which he sold his own estate went into the fund) and to gather the adventurous Puritan spirits who would populate the colony.

When they were gathered, they numbered nearly 1,000 people—the most numerous emigration that Britain had so far managed to produce. Historians have conferred on many mass movements out of these islands the distinctive title of 'the great migration': here was the first of them. The emigrants came from all over England—the majority from London and East Anglia, about 150 from the West Country, a sizeable contingent from Northamptonshire and Lincolnshire, and handfuls from Yorkshire, Lancashire, Kent, Leicestershire, Gloucestershire and more. They included a handful of gentry and of that fairly new phenomenon, the middle class; all the rest were carefully recruited artisans, tradesmen and farmers with their wives and families. Of the artisans and skilled workers it is worth noting that the party included about five blacksmiths and the same number of carpenters and bakers, about three tailors and physicians, two masons and only one tanner. Not all the 1,000 emigrants were devoted to the Puritan cause, it must be made clear, but all were certainly 'screened' for a sufficient degree of piety—and therefore perhaps for the potentiality of conversion to the Puritan way.

In March 1630 they sailed from Cowes in eleven ships, amply supplied with livestock and necessary pioneering equipment. Each adult had paid the Bay Company £5 passage, an all-in payment that included fare and provisions during the voyage. Children went at reduced rates, and there was a charge of £4 a ton for goods and possessions. Clearly, then, these were people of substance—if the head of an average family could lay out £20 or £30 for the crossing, aside from other preparatory expenses. For the less well off and for hired labourers, special arrangements allowed them to pay only a part of the fare and to undertake to work in New England at three shillings a day to pay the remainder.

The great Puritan divine John Cotton, minister of Boston in Lincolnshire and a principal spiritual mainstay of the entire emigration, had at one point come down to Southampton to preach to the assembling emigrants and to pray for their safety. Undoubtedly most of them believed that such intercession smoothed their passage—for the voyage progressed swiftly, and everyone survived without too much discomfort. Winthrop noted a few 'stiff' or 'handsome' April gales, much rain, and one storm that lasted for several days during which time about seventy cattle on one ship died from being excessively thrown about. But other-

wise there was no especial or unusual unpleasantness, and
the fleet arrived in June, in excellent time to make a start
on preparing shelter and provision against the winter.
Endecott and the rest of the advance guard at Salem had
erected a number of houses, had stored up grain and other
supplies of food; and the Puritan emigrants were greeted
not only with calm offshore waters and fishing that produced cod 'a yard and a half long', as Winthrop marvelled,
but with a delightful colonial feast in Salem of venison
pasty, good beer and wild strawberries. Then Winthrop
injected an inspirational note into the joys of the landing,
with his famous and often-quoted statement of a colonial
dream which was to come true:

> ...we shall be as a city upon a hill, the eyes of all
> people are upon us; so that if we shall deal falsely
> with our God in this work we have undertaken and so
> cause him to withdraw his present help from us, we
> shall be made a story and a byword through the world.

As it happened, in spite of the general mood, some of the
emigrants seemed to think as they reached Massachusetts
Bay that God's help had long been absent from the enterprise. They saw the preparations at Salem as merely a
clutch of crude huts, and the fields as merely a few hoe-
marks on the wilderness. Some of them understandably
interpreted this sight as an invitation to famine, and
promptly got back onto the ships and went back to England. Winthrop decried their faint hearts, and certainly
perceived a providential irony when the returning ships
were badly mauled, and many returnees killed, in a combination of Atlantic storms and an attack by Spanish
vessels.

For those who stayed, there was the blessing of New
England summer weather, the usual natural abundance
of fruit, game and seafood, and a notable scarcity of Indians
in the locality, which Winthrop rightly ascribed to smallpox and which he considered, as the Pilgrims had in their
turn, to be a further example of God's beneficence upon
their enterprise. (Puritan belief was never noted for putting
any stock in God's mercy or forgiveness.) Within this atmosphere, the leaders got down to the task of choosing the
exact site for their home, for they seem to have concluded

that Salem would not be roomy enough nor the soil fit enough. At first they considered the minute hamlet of Charlestown, built on the Charles river by some of Endecott's pioneers, and there they settled down to the labours of building habitation for themselves against the winter to come.

The colonists set to with a will, though by then food supplies were vanishing rapidly down the many hundreds of throats, even though supplemented by many a fish and clam. Of course they had to build a meeting house first, for worship, so that many of the newcomers were still housed in sailcloth tents when winter arrived in full force, while others spent most of the winter in their versions of the Indian 'wigwam'—pliable poles stuck into the ground and bent to form a crude dome shape, fastened together to make a frame over which skins, mats, canvas, even thatching might be spread. With such poor shelter, the first New England winter proved murderous, as first winters there usually did. Inadequate food brought malnutrition and scurvy, which further weakened the exhausted and frozen people. The strongest among them, men and women, waded daily into the freezing sea to dig deep for shellfish, while others plodded through the snow to Plymouth to trade what they could with the sympathetic Pilgrims for a few packs of corn.

Two hundred out of Winthrop's party died that winter —and no doubt the toll would have been far worse if, back in July, Winthrop had not foreseen the danger of mid-winter starvation. He had then sensibly contracted with one of the ship's captains to bring a cargo of supplies—and in the dark beginnings of February, when many Puritan families were nibbling the last stale remains of bread baked with their last bit of corn meal, the good ship *Lion* sailed in loaded with beef, bread, beer and lemons against the scurvy.

So they survived, and were able to plunge into work again when spring arrived—fortuitously early. At that point the leaders reached the decision that Charlestown's water was not as sweet as it might be, and the colony cheerfully picked up what could be carried from the previous autumn's labours and moved everything to a new site, across the river, where there was good water, a fine sheltered harbour, and some high ground that could with a little stretching of the imagination allow them to anticipate Winthrop's 'city upon a hill'. They named it Boston.

Its only disadvantage was a lack of timber ready to hand, which slowed the rate of building and increased its laboriousness—so that for some years the typical residence of a Bostonian was a one-room shack built of crude boards. The predecessors of the Winthrop fleet had dug 'sawpits' as an early priority so as to cut boards and planks, and Winthrop's people followed that example. A small brickworks had also got started at Salem, but served only to provide brick fireplaces for the more substantial settler homes. Such homes, too, might have as their exterior cladding the comparative refinement of clapboard, when the carpenters among the emigrants got to work; but just as often a house would present an exterior of plain weatherboarding—ordinary boards nailed horizontally to the frame, overlapping each other.

Inside, fairly crude plaster would be the order of the day, with whitewash when available; windows would be of diamond-pane glass brought carefully from England. The wives would scrub floorboards white with sand and home-made soft soap, and those who had them would add a touch of homeliness with cushions, hangings and the like. But generally an interior would be dominated by the huge crude fireplace (with an oven built in, within which the wife first had to lay a fire and then clear it out when the bricks were hot enough for baking) and by the equally plain and rough home-made furniture, limited in quantity as well as quality. Such generally drab interiors, dimly lit at night with tallow candles, combined badly with the exteriors, which would not taste paint for generations, and which were surrounded by muddy meandering paths garnished with heaps of carelessly discarded household rubbish and assorted livestock.

Yet if the colony's outward appearance gave the impression of being pinched, dingy and depressed, the mood that seemed to prevail there was one of hearty determination and ambition—once the more faint-hearted of the first emigrants had returned home. From the outset the keynote of the Massachusetts Bay Colony was growth. It grew because the increasingly dangerous situation in England was driving more and more Puritans to take advantage of Winthrop's path-clearing. And it grew because, given population pressures and general tendencies to be footloose, the emigrants began to expand into new ground.

Winthrop's fleet had brought 1,000 people to the Bay in 1630; the next year further groups of ships brought a total of 2,000 more English emigrants. And these mass departures went on, in ensuing years—not always maintaining the same annual level, though, so that in 1633 only about 700 sailed for Massachusetts, while in 1638 New England's population was swollen by about 3,000. All in all, during those darkening years from 1630 to the initiation of the Long Parliament in 1642, approximately 20,000 people emigrated from England and became Massachusetts Bay Colonists.

So over a mere ten years the tiny wilderness outpost of the Pilgrims had been a dozen times overshadowed by the larger collection of outposts that housed the Puritans. But it must be re-emphasized here that by no means all of those 20,000 new arrivals were devout members of the Puritan church. Most estimates suggest that the true Puritans were a dominant minority, perhaps numbering about 4,000—dominant because it was from them exclusively that the tiny group was chosen to form the entire colony's oligarchic government, the General Court set up in the charter. The rest of the thousands joined in this ten-year 'great migration' for a variety of reasons other than common religious dissent. Clearly many of them, even if they did not follow Puritan doctrine every step of the way, shared with the Puritans some measure of distaste for the leanings towards the Church of Rome being shown by Charles and by his new Archbishop of Canterbury, William Laud, sworn and zealous enemy of dissenters, whose persecutions no doubt helped to swell the size of the emigration. Certainly many of the emigrants of the time left home for the same reasons that some emigrants would always leave home: to seek adventure, to make their fortune in some faraway land of opportunity, to escape debts or other embarrassments. And the call of almost infinitely abundant free land would be insuperably magnetic to many independent-minded farmers, especially when men like Captain John Smith were heard to speak of this colonial land so highly. Moreover, non-Puritan men of substance found their incomes sharply dwindling in real value as Charles's machinations damaged the economy, while craftsmen and tradesmen found their skills put to less and less remunerative use, as unemployment reached new heights. Politically minded men packed up and left a country where a badly advised king was exerting himself to wrench all political power out of the hands of the people, thereby moving towards the kind of autocracy that could lead only to strife and violence. 'The world's in a heap of troubles and confusion,' said one emigrant (quoted by David Hawke), 'and while they are in the midst of their changes and amazes, the best way... is to go out of the world and leave them'.

So the most startling mass exodus of Englishmen in England's history till then found its varied reasons and impulsions. Not that it was so large in terms of later movements: but it took place at a time when colonies were still novelties and emigration to colonies an unimaginably adventurous and hazardous undertaking. In this context, the size of the exodus is more impressive. And it must be added that even more Englishmen emigrated to other shores than the 20,000 who became New Englanders: by 1640 Virginia possessed a population of 8,000, Maryland had reached past 1,500, and the various settlements in the West Indies had attracted (in a conservative estimate) upwards of 40,000 people who had 'gone out of the world' and its upheavals.

In New England, as noted, this massive injection of population put tremendous pressure on the *liebensraum* of the Bay Colony. But, for that matter, even from the start with the arrival of Winthrop's 1,000 there had been a certain amount of pressure on space. Certainly not every one of the emigrants from the original fleet chose to crowd into Boston on their governor's heels. Some stayed on in Salem; others stayed in Charlestown instead of making the shift to Boston. And, after the capital's establishment had begun, others began to show some of the first hints in New England of what would become traditional Yankee restlessness. When Winthrop created a farm for himself at Medford, some of the colonists joined him at that site. Others went out on their own, looking for even more suitable sites than Boston, seeking more timber, perhaps, or richer soil—for there was a preponderance of thin, sandy, rock-strewn land within the Colony, as indeed there would prove to be throughout most of the New England colonies.

## The Puritan Flight

So there rapidly grew up around Boston the satellite hamlets, built by men of the Winthrop fleet, of Watertown, Dorchester, Roxbury and Newtown which would later be renamed Cambridge. The village of Weymouth, established in 1624 down the coast somewhat from Boston (see Chapter 2), attracted a few Massachusetts Bay settlers; so did the small trading post built northwards on the Bay in 1629 by a group mainly from Lincolnshire, and later to be named Lynn. As the other thousands flowed into the Bay in the ensuing decade, these clutches of little huts burgeoned into towns, and spawned new satellites of their own—as when Salem men went out to build Topsfield (first called New Meadows), when Lynn gave birth to Reading, Sandwich and Yarmouth, when Watertown people settled Dedham, all in the 1630s. But the newer arrivals did their own exploring, too, and chose their own sites for brand-new Massachusetts villages: Ipswich, where John Winthrop Jnr lent a hand in 1633, and Hingham sprang up rich in Norfolk emigrants; a Yorkshire minister brought a sizeable congregation who erected the village of Rowley in 1638; in 1635 a peaceful transaction with local Indians, in which some newcomers bought an inland site, so impressed the buyers that they named their village Concord—which was the first Massachusetts settlement not situated within easy reach of tide-water. (The Puritan emigrants' tendency to cling together in villages and towns—rather than to scatter across the land in more separated farms as often happened in other frontiers—was not because of an undue terror of the wilderness, but because they had generally emigrated in groups, whether congregations or whole parishes, and these tended to stay together.)

By the mid-thirties, as these towns mushroomed along the coast, and as the ships continued landing with their thousands of passengers, the Bay Colony was bursting at the seams—that is, the Colony as described in the charter, which established the boundaries at a line three miles north of the Merrimac river, and another three miles south of the Charles river. Unfortunately, the people who drew up the charter apparently did not realize that these uncooperative rivers did not run neatly west to east: the Merrimac runs north to south before turning sharply eastward for its last few miles. The difficulty, then, of establishing the exact position of the ordained boundary gave the colonists some excuse—not that they badly needed one—for ignoring boundaries and forcing their way into wilderness well away from Massachusetts Bay, there to lay the groundwork for the rest of New England. Many of these adventurous pioneers left the Bay simply to find a better, more fertile and spacious place to live than the crowded environs of Boston and the other towns could provide. Some, though, left because they found life under the Puritan oligarchs intolerable—or indeed because they were driven out.

The seekers after richer land had some of their prayers answered when information (brought by Indians) filtered through the colony about the superb fertility of the Connecticut river valley. The Indians were in fact playing power politics: the smaller tribes of that valley (including the last of the Mohicans, led by the wily Uncas whom Fenimore Cooper chose as his model of the noble savage) were all under the heel of the dangerous Pequots, to whom they paid a stiff tribute. Mohican representatives visited the new colonies, Massachusetts and Plymouth, to suggest English trading expeditions to the Connecticut—hoping that such a trade could be used to dislodge the Pequots from their dominance. The Plymouth colonists were interested, and Edward Winslow, who by then had explored the Kennebec, went in 1632 to look also at the Connecticut.

He returned full of good reports about both land and trading possibilities, and on that basis the Pilgrims suggested to Massachusetts that they launch a large joint trading expedition. The Bay Colony turned down the idea. Then in 1634 a stormy character named John Oldham, once a Plymouth 'stranger' but ejected forcibly from that colony some time earlier for his rebellious trouble-making, wandered down to the Connecticut to trade, and brought back further good reports to Watertown in Massachusetts. It had become fairly clear by this time that the Bay Colony had refused the Plymouth suggestion of a joint expedition because they wanted the Connecticut for their own. In any case, the Bay colonists soon asserted themselves in the Connecticut valley.

They were led to do so partly because the Dutch from the Hudson valley had earlier made an appearance along the Connecticut, and—in the face of the potential threat from the English—had erected in 1633 a small fort near the river's mouth. But the commander of the fort lacked the courage of his annexations, and did nothing when a further group of explorers from Plymouth sailed aggressively past the fort and on upriver, there to establish a trading post on lands bought from the Mohicans. (So in one stroke the English colonists had angered the Dutch and antagonized the Pequots, who felt the Pilgrims should have paid *them* for the land.) All this sudden activity in the valley was then increased further by new intrusions in 1635, from Massachusetts, and direct from England.

The Massachusetts newcomers came mostly from Dorchester, Newtown and Watertown—colonists hungry for good land and careless about how they got it, but loudly asserting that their charter gave them some rights on the upper Connecticut because of the way the Charles river twisted. The Bay Colonists did not merely settle on land near the Plymouth trading post; perversely, they insisted on settling on the *same* land, ignoring Pilgrim protestations that those rich meadows of the upper river valley had been properly bought by them from the Mohicans. In 1637, after much wrangling, the Bay Colony would grudgingly pay £37 compensation to Plymouth; but for the time being they had performed, and got away with, a miniature invasion.

They remained just as high-handed when a small party of men came out from England in 1635 to undertake, it seems, a small and entirely private colonizing venture. Complex land dealings in England, involving the Council for New England, had resulted in a huge grant of New England land to the Earl of Warwick, who in turn issued sub-grants, as it were. One of these—for land on the upper Connecticut—came to Sir Richard Saltonstall, one of the Massachusetts Bay Company founders. He sent out twenty men to build a colony on his land. Unfortunately, the colonists from Dorchester and the rest were on that patch first—and Saltonstall's colonists received as short shrift as the Pilgrims had done.

The site that had been so rudely annexed by the Dorchester emigrants was to become the village of Windsor—even though the furies of the first winter very nearly killed it at birth. Curiously, although it was an early winter as well as a fierce one, a group of fifty to sixty men, women and children from Newtown (Cambridge) had decided as late as October to join the exodus to the Connecticut, and —sending possessions and supplies round by water—had marched overland to establish themselves down river from Windsor, and so to form the first beginnings of Hartford. Then the winter struck, and the migration went into reverse. The river froze earlier than usual, supplies could not reach the settlements, and most of the land-seekers fled back to the Bay—overland if they could, or making their way downriver to find water transport from the rivermouth around to Boston.

Still, a few hardy souls remained behind, their survival aided by friendly Indians, to maintain the continuity of the new Connecticut settlements. When spring finally struck through the snow and ice most of the previous emigrants to Connecticut returned, to carry on with the start they had made in their pioneering. And they were joined by still others—presumably drawn by the winter's reports of fine land—so that in 1636 the embryonic colony of Connecticut held 800 people, mostly in the villages of Hartford, Windsor and Wethersfield, but with a few new houses on a nearby site called Agawam, later renamed Springfield.

A potential source of complication, however, had arisen in the previous autumn when representatives of a group of English noblemen had arrived to lay claim to the Connecticut river lands. This group, including Lord Brook and Lord Saye and Sele, had like Saltonstall acquired land through a patent in 1632 from the Earl of Warwick; the representatives they sent were led by John Winthrop Jnr, eldest son of the Massachusetts leader. Their object was to found a new and separate colony that would be of sufficient quality and comfort to be used as a refuge for hard-pressed Puritan noblemen whom Charles might harass into emigration. No doubt young Winthrop's presence ensured peaceful agreement between the rightful owners of 'Saybrook', as the lordly colony was to be called, and the squatters from Massachusetts, which is what they were. The English group built a fort at the mouth of the river, mainly to give the Dutch pause, grandly allowed the squatters to remain, but then sat within their fort and engaged in no further colony building. Nor did any of the potentially emigrant nobles ever tear themselves away from their English preoccupations, though their Puritan connections came to make life more and more difficult for them. So Saybrook

remained an obscure little fort tasting importance only
once, and briefly, in later years when it was rumoured that
Cromwell himself might emigrate there.

Predictably, then, the governance of the new colony, as
Connecticut could now be fairly called, fell upon the more
authoritative emigrés from Massachusetts. And none was
more able to bear the burden than a stern and powerful
preacher named Thomas Hooker, one of the most important and influential Puritan clergymen, who had emigrated
to New England—with his entire congregation—in 1633.
Coincidentally, in the same batch of new arrivals came
another Puritan divine who was, if anything, even more
widely known and influential: John Cotton, the inspiring
and spiritually guiding force for the Massachusetts emigrants from the first conception of their plan. In normal
circumstances, Massachusetts would probably not have
been big enough for both of these men. But Hooker, who
settled with his people at Newtown, was even more bound
to conflict with Cotton and the Boston oligarchy, for he
had strong and definite ideas about how people should be
governed, and oligarchy did not form a part of them. His
most famous remark—famous in the annals of the American
democratic process—asserted that regarding 'matters that
concern the common good' the political institution 'most
suitable to rule' would be

a general council, chosen by all, to transact business
which concerns all. ...

Naturally the key words 'chosen by all' do not necessarily imply full democracy as we know it, or think we
know it; but they were radical enough to make some sort
of collision inevitable. After an exchange of contentious
sermons with Cotton, Hooker took his people in the spring
of 1636 and marched them—more than one hundred
people, about seventy of whom were women and children
—along an overland Indian trail towards Connecticut.
Burdened with possessions, though heavier goods went
round by water, driving 160 cattle and many swine before
them on narrow paths that most of the time were imper-
ceptible in the heavy forest, navigating by compass alone,
throwing together dubious rafts to cross the rivers they
met, their skin torn and slashed by 'the thickets, where their

hands are forced to make way for their bodies' passage, and their feet clambering over the crossed trees . . .', sweltering in the summer heat, making about ten miles a day and sleeping on the bare ground at night, they stumbled into Hartford after two weeks of travel.

Within a year Hooker had so imposed his views on the scattering of Connecticut villages, including the garrison at the fort of Saybrook, that they had formed a sort of unity within their agreement to choose—through what Hooker called 'the free consent of the people'—their own General Court to decide matters of common interest. By 1639 they would have drawn up an *ad hoc* constitution called the 'Fundamental Orders of Connecticut' which made clear the fact that Massachusetts' daughter colony had grown up and was standing on her own two feet.

By that time, due to further religious controversy akin to Hooker's but much more fiery and disruptive, another daughter colony had sprung up, even if the family relationship was not always acknowledged. This severance arose from the presence in New England of a strong-minded minister named Roger Williams. Of Welsh origins and a brilliant preacher, Williams held enough radical beliefs to ensure a cloud over him in Puritan Massachusetts almost immediately upon his arrival among the emigrants of 1631. He upset the Puritan establishment with his passionate separatist feelings: and, at a time when powerful forces in England (Archbishop Laud among them) were seeking somehow to undermine the Puritan colonization, the Boston leaders knew it was no time to provide ammunition to the enemy with talk of severing relations with the Church of England. Attempts were made to hush Williams up; he replied with more subversive statements, among them the notion that the *civil* authorities should have no right to punish breaches of *religious* tenets. That struck at the very root of the Puritan oligarchy's control, firmly based on the idea that the best government was a theocracy combining religious and secular rule. At last perceiving that he had made few friends in Boston, Williams took himself to be minister at Salem, which town received a sharp condemnation from Boston for inviting him. From then on the pressure on Salem increased, until Williams moved out of Massachusetts entirely—and went to Plymouth.

Presumably the separatist 'saints' did not find him so

hard to take at the outset, but during his three years there he managed to raise a good many hackles—as when he preached on the mistreatment of the Indians, and the questionable legality of colonial 'patents' allowing the occupation of the Indians' land. That was a special sore point with the Pilgrims, whose patent was shakier than most. Shortly Williams was back at Salem, captivating congregations with his magnetic sermons but unnerving them with his radicalism. Now he was saying (to oversimplify drastically) that points of religious doctrine ought to be the concern of the individual, not imposed by authority. In other words, he was preaching religious *toleration*—anathema to the Puritan way of things. That was apparently as far as he could be allowed to go. In late 1636 he was brought before the Massachusetts court, tried reasonably fairly for his anti-authoritarianism, and sentenced to be banished from the colony.

The sentence was to be carried out the following spring, but then the authorities awoke to the danger that if Williams went elsewhere in the New England wilderness, perhaps to found a colony of his own, he would be a potential source of religious 'infection'. So they decided to ship him back to England. Williams got wind of the plan, thanks to the kindly sympathy of Winthrop, and in the depths of January he slipped away from the settlement into the frozen wilderness—with a minimum of supplies and equipment, weakened by illness, but borne up by the company of four young men from Salem who chose to share his exile. 'Sorely tossed for fourteen weeks in a bitter winter season, not knowing what bread or bed did mean,' Williams made his way to the Narragansett region where he and his companions began to make what few preliminary scratchings they could towards a settlement, at a site called Seekonk. But shortly a note—firm though not unfriendly—arrived from Plymouth. Seekonk was unfortunately on Pilgrim territory; while the Pilgrims would not object to a Williams colony as a neighbour, they preferred such a place to be outside that patent of theirs which he called into question. So Williams and his associates picked up and moved across Narragansett Bay, where they began again to build a settlement. This time they built on land given them by the Narragansett Indians—who were mightily feared by the Puritans, but with

whom Williams struck up a friendship—thanks largely
to his enlightened view of the Indian's rights in his own
land—that was to last through all the violent and bloody
years to come. Properly, Williams called his new settlement Providence—and from the start established within
it a considerable range of civil liberty and almost total religious tolerance.

The presence of such a colony in New England made it
an ideal refuge for others, later, who came into conflict
with the established Puritan orthodoxy. Most notable
among these was Anne Hutchinson, a former parishioner
of John Cotton's who emigrated with her husband in 1634
—and whose initial 'dismay' at the external appearance of
Boston town soon gave way to a dedication to Puritan piety
that approached mysticism. Naturally in the seventeenth
century women did not become preachers—but within an
intimate circle of women friends Anne Hutchinson soon
gained prominence as a magnetic and rewarding explicator
of religious doctrine. By 1636 her audience had expanded
to include almost half the population of Boston, and had
created a fearful split within the colony. It was political as
well as religious, as shown when one of her followers, young
Henry Vane, the brilliant twenty-six-year-old who arrived
with Winthrop Junior, joined in 1636 the line of succession from Winthrop Senior by being elected governor.

In terms of religion, the split caused by Mrs Hutchinson's influence arose from her somewhat imprecisely expressed concept that the grace of God could become manifest to the individual, somehow circumventing the need for
a preacher interpreting the Scriptures—with all the extras
of church authority, religious discipline, rigid moral and
doctrinal laws and the other totalitarian corollaries to the
'official' interpretation. In other words, the individual
could have a *direct line* to God, without any need of the
Puritan power structure. Naturally the theocracy moved
against her and against the 'Antinomian' (roughly, 'anti-
law') movement that had grown up around her, gathering
to it all colonists who had some grudge—religious, political,
financial, personal—against the Puritan establishment.

As an initial stroke, the hard-core Puritans manoeuvred
Winthrop back into office, displacing Vane. As another,
they secured a recantation from the great John Cotton,
who had apparently been swayed to some degree by Anne

Hutchinson. Thus strengthened, the establishment brought together a 'synod' of ministers in 1637 and raised up that ugly word *heresy*, in whose name so many horrors had been and were to be committed. Out of the machinations of the General Court and this synod, several momentous achievements occurred. An immigration law was framed, forbidding, in essence, any Englishman settling in Massachusetts without express permission of the Court (that is, the oligarchy). And at the same time a number of leading Antinomians were tried for religious error, found guilty and banished.

Ultimately, as the establishment faction grew more secure with these victories, it brought Anne Hutchinson herself to trial—and the result was easily forecast. She too was banished, and in 1638 left Massachusetts—following more or less in Roger Williams' footsteps, to found a colony of her own, with her family and many supporters who remained faithful, called Portsmouth, on Narragansett Bay. Years later she and other members of her embryonic colony moved again, to live within New Amsterdam—and there they were massacred by Indians in 1643. The grimly self-righteous Puritans of Massachusetts saw this, as they had seen a miscarriage she had had while among them, as God's retribution, and a justification of their actions.

The same spring when Anne Hutchinson moved to Narragansett Bay, some eighteen Antinomians who had earlier left Massachusetts to try colonizing a site in Maine decided that winters so far north were too uncomfortable, and also moved down to join the other exiles from Massachusetts. Various conflicts and ambitions within the groups around Portsmouth led to more hivings-off, so that one smaller group, led by a Hutchinsonian named William Coddington, left to found Newport in 1639, while a persistent trouble-maker named Samuel Gorton, who had been expelled from almost every other New England colony, set up his own settlement and called it Warwick. For years all these early beginnings of Rhode Island remained wholly separate and highly suspicious of each other and of their larger neighbours, Massachusetts and Connecticut.

As for the latter, it was potentially enlarged further by the arrival in 1637 of an extremely solid and moneyed set of emigrants. At their head was a rigidly doctrinaire Puritan minister, John Davenport of London, and a wealthy

Puritan merchant and parishioner of Davenport's, Theophilus Eaton. They brought with them 250 disaffected
Puritans who found the growing harassment of their
co-believers intolerable, and who had decided to found a
colony with the minimum of pioneering discomfort, by
virtue of the maximum of financial preparation. The group
included many other men of substance, and many professional men, including the father of the man who was to
found Yale University.

This sturdy group decided against the environs of
Boston, partly no doubt because of the religious 'laxity'
which they read into the Antinomian struggles then taking
place. They heard reports of the excellence of the harbour
land on the Quinnipiac Bay, south of the Connecticut,
and there they moved to buy land from the Indians and
set up their rich little town, which they named New Haven.
The construction of the town was something of a marvel
in those colonial days, with its spacious and comfortable
houses: Eaton's house reportedly held nineteen fireplaces,
while Davenport's had thirteen. The commercial possibilities of the bay, backed by New Haven capital, attracted
other emigrants, like the party of forty who settled in 1639
on a nearby site and called it Guilford, or the similar group
who called their nearby settlement Milford. But these
potentially separate settlements had by 1643 been absorbed
into the colony of New Haven. New Haven in its turn
would eventually be swallowed by Connecticut—and, rather
like the image of a sequence of fish each of which is eating
a smaller and being eaten by a larger, Connecticut always
fearfully looked over its shoulder at the biggest fish, Massachusetts. Equally afraid of that hunger, and for good reason
as will be seen, were the new nuclei of settlements to the
north—in New Hampshire and Maine.

Back in the early 1620s, in another of those confusing
parcellings-out of New England that might well have
managed to Balkanize the whole region, the Council for
New England had generously granted to Sir Ferdinando
Gorges and his business associate John Mason the whole
territory—then all called Maine—between the Merrimac
river and the Kennebec. In 1629 the two men had divided
their land between them, Mason taking the western portion,
calling it New Hampshire, and Gorges taking the eastern
portion to be known as Maine. New Hampshire by then

already held a few minute establishments—including a short-lived one on the coast slightly south of the Piscataqua river, and another which would become the town of Dover inland on that river, the latter founded by two fishmonger brothers from London named Hilton. Mason backed another settlement in that area, apparently with some unfounded hopes of mineral wealth, and by the time of his death in 1635 Piscataqua seems to have been fairly substantial, boasting considerable livestock, fishing boats and other signs of progress. The residents tended to be fairly conformist in their C. of E. religion, which kept them apart from the Bay Colony—and from the Puritan leanings shown at Dover, especially after some of the Puritan lords in the Council for New England bought out the Hilton interest and sent over Puritan colonists, who were joined in the late 1630s by some Antinomian refugees from Boston.

A considerably more important Antinomian—namely Anne Hutchinson's brother-in-law John Wheelwright, banished with her from Massachusetts—came to New Hampshire in 1638 and with thirty-five companions built the settlement of Exeter there. At that point Massachusetts began again to demonstrate its general appetite for expansion. The oligarchy officially sanctioned the beginnings of a settlement beyond the Merrimac boundary, peopled by fifty-six emigrants mainly from Norfolk. It later acquired the name Hampton, and became the Bay Colony's possession in New Hampshire that would serve as nine-tenths of the law. John Mason, ostensible holder of proprietary rights in the area, had died in 1635, and no one else in England seemed interested. So the isolated little New Hampshire hamlets bowed to the inevitable and in the 1640s allowed themselves to be absorbed by Massachusetts, in which they would remain until 1677.

When Exeter was swallowed Wheelwright had once again to move, and sought a refuge in Gorges' Maine, where he founded a settlement named Wells. In Maine the fishing and fur trading industries had spawned a few other tiny and isolated patches of settlement, like that set up in 1623 in Casco Bay, or the Pilgrim trading post on the Kennebec—which was the scene of a notorious shooting affray in 1634 when a trespassing trader killed one of the Pilgrim traders and was promptly shot in turn by another man from Plymouth. None of these establishments were yet sizeable enough to attract Massachusetts' annexation-prone interest, but they interested Gorges: he had previously sought to be governor (indeed, virtually viceroy) of the whole of New England—and in 1639 he acquired a royal charter that allowed him to play the autocrat within Maine. He could legislate, control trade and fishing rights, could even create manorial courts. Of course Gorges, by then quite elderly, played out this feudal game from the safe confines of England until his death in the 1650s. By then Massachusetts would be successfully pressing its claim to Maine, which it would in time entirely engulf. But in 1640 it was less than concerned with the assortment of wild fishermen and transient traders who made up the bulk of Maine's few hundred population—in a year when Connecticut held 2,000, the Rhode Island villages 300 among them, and the breadth of Massachusetts 14,000.

In years to come, as civil war in England put an end to the drain of Puritan emigration, natural increase would provide by far the bulk of any further growth of population. Indeed, many New England Puritans went home to play their parts in constructing the Commonwealth. Those that remained in New England turned their concentration inwards, onto colonial matters. Even so, they did not want for unrest, discord and strife.

# 4. Interregnum: Expansion and Oppression

The territorial expansion of New England would always seem more or less uninhibited, but perhaps never more so than in that first decade of the great Puritan emigration. And yet, even though Massachusetts and its sister colonies seemed highly skilled at evading threats to their growth, or steamrollering over potential opposition, no one should overlook the fact that such threat and hindrance existed plentifully, and were of the sort that might have wrecked less determined colonies before they were fairly started. It has been seen how Massachusetts dealt with the religious dissension of Roger Williams and others, which, to the Puritan leaders, was certainly the most heinous sort of threat to the colony's future. But at about the same time there had been an external danger that led to violence and bloodshed—and to clear demonstration, if that were necessary, of the Puritan oligarchy's ruthless determination to survive.

Remember that the thin edge of the settlers' wedge entered Connecticut because of trouble between local river Indians and the fierce Pequot tribe, pushing in from the Hudson river region, threatening the Mohicans of Uncas, the Narragansetts and other tribes. Eventually (Bradford suggests it was because they were 'puffed up with many victories') the Pequots began also to threaten the whites, who were expanding aggressively into the disputed territory. Storm warnings became visible in isolated incidents—the early killing of a Virginian trader who was operating in the Connecticut forests, then in 1635 the massacre of John Oldham, another trader formerly of Plymouth (see page 46. Massachusetts, or its leaders, apparently fell into an unreasoning fury, and sent John Endecott with ninety men on a punitive expedition, with orders to show no mercy. They were to go to the river island where Oldham had been murdered, and they were to kill the Pequot men and make the women and children captives.

In the event, the Pequots vanished into the underbrush and Endecott's party resorted valiantly to burning wigwams and slaughtering dogs. They then proceeded by boat to the main Pequot encampment, issued a provocative combination of threats and demands for compensation that the chiefs had to reject, then performed the same destructive assault while those Indians too disappeared into the woods.

So began the Pequot war, with the Indians taking the offensive through 1636 in a series of scattered, woodcrafty raids against the colonists. Ironically, when Boston heard that the Pequots were seeking an alliance with the Narragansetts to bring about a general Indian rising, the oligarchy had to swallow its pride and seek help from Roger Williams, who had always maintained the most serenely friendly relations with the Indians of his region. Williams brought his diplomatic skills to the rescue and kept the Narragansetts out of the war, at some considerable risk to his life from the Pequots.

By spring 1637 the Puritans had gathered themselves for a massive reprisal against the Pequots—reprisal for the thirty whites who had by then been killed in the guerrilla raiding. It was to have been a unified thrust, but intercolonial co-operation was not at its best, and Connecticut—with some help from Uncas—launched the attack on its own. It was aimed at an important Pequot fort on the Mystic river, which seemed rather poorly guarded by the over-confident Indians, for the Puritan forces were inside the log palisades before the Pequots knew they were being attacked. After some inconclusive hand-to-hand fighting, the whites set fire to the fort, withdrew and surrounded it, and shot at any Indian trying to escape the flames. A conservative estimate of the time said that about 400 Pequots, including women and children, died that night one way or the other. Only two Puritans were killed, though about forty Mohicans died, probably because the whites had not always distinguished them clearly enough from Pequots.

This slaughter shattered the Pequot aggression, and the rest of the war consisted of moppings-up, during which several hundred more Pequot men were killed. By the end

*An early nineteenth-century conception of the massacre of the Indians during the Pequot War*

of it the tribe had been nearly exterminated; other tribes, thoroughly impressed, were nervously assuring the Puritans of their undying friendship; and of course the Connecticut valley had been opened wide for wholesale overrunning by land-hungry Puritans.

At the same time, the Bay Colony was engaged in another struggle, against the Antinomian enemy within, which was noted in Chapter 3—and also to a lesser extent against a burgeoning, if still weak, groundswell of demand by the colonists for some check on the theocracy's power and some general liberalization. To worsen the atmosphere of crisis, there had also been a serious threat from abroad, when Archbishop Laud—Charles's powerful arm in the growing assault on Puritanism—had in the 1630s demanded to see Massachusetts' charter, only to find that it had gone to New England, symbolizing the transfer of the Bay Company's management and the colony's government out of England. When orders came from England to return the charter, Massachusetts replied with the sort of delays and evasions—neither compliance nor outright refusal—which it would so often employ to retain its autonomy. And the delaying actions served their purpose, for as the 1640s began the English authorities had become too embroiled in their domestic disputes and oppressions to spare time for disciplining a faraway colony, however arrogant it might have become in its assumption of near-independence.

As for the yearning among the colonists for a measure of liberalization, it was mostly expressed by those who were not hardline Puritans and who were therefore (though in the majority) disfranchised and almost powerless. By the early 1640s, though, the General Court had offered a sop to their desire to have a say in colonial affairs, by allowing the towns of Massachusetts to send 'deputies' to the Court, forming a kind of House of Commons debating society while the oligarchs (corresponding to the Cabinet) made the decisions and held the power. Still, the deputies provided some focus for the reforming urge within public opinion—as when in 1644 the people wanted an extension of what were even then called 'civil liberties' to all residents whether or not they were Puritan church members. In essence they were asking for no more than those rights which they would have held at home in England. But the theocrats, smelling subversion, made no more placatory concessions: they accused the petitioners, McCarthy-style, of trying to undermine the colony; and they fined them heavily and threw the leaders into prison.

In those troubled years, as mentioned before, emigration had almost come to a halt. Most people then ascribed the damming of the flow after 1640 to the brightening outlook for Puritans in England as the Long Parliament took its seats and Charles and his Cavaliers began their losing battle. In Winthrop's words, this 'general reformation both of church and state ... caused all men to stay in England in expectation of a new world'. But some of the worst intolerances of New England, damaging the image of the real New World, certainly contributed to the dwindling of emigration to those shores. Even the friends of Massachusetts, like the Earl of Warwick or Lord Saye and Sele, had objected to some of the colony's high-handed ways. Lord Saye had indeed begun sending Puritan emigrants (before 1640) to the West Indies instead—where, in 1641, several hundred non-Puritan New Englanders also chose to go, to escape further intolerance.

The cessation of emigration, and the almost total severance of links with England during the upheaval of the civil war, led to a worsening of the situation in New England, for everyone but the oligarchs. With no newcomers bringing in badly needed currency with which they would buy the surplus produce of established settlers, the New England economy went into the doldrums. This proved a more worrisome threat to colonial stability than had the previous reformist ferment within or the clash with the English authorities. Furthermore, New England was also worrying about the strengthening Dutch and French presences to the south and north respectively, and there were rumours of new stirrings among the Indians, especially the Narragansetts.

Out of these disturbances came discussion among the colonies' leaders of some kind of unity from which to gain strength, in defence and in mutual economic shoring-up. The idea came from the Connecticut towns, but they were not so fearful for their security that they would let themselves fall into the maw of Massachusetts. They proposed a *federal* union, with each colony retaining some autonomy and having an equal voice within the federation. Massachusetts eventually accepted the idea, but rigorously re-

jected any possibility that the towns of Maine would gain
admission and thereby recognition of their separate iden-
tity. Those frontier hamlets were frowned upon for religious laxity—besides which, and more importantly,
Massachusetts had every intention of absorbing them, as it
soon would.

So the four larger colonies—Massachusetts, Connecticut,
Plymouth and New Haven—came together in 1643 as the
United Colonies of New England, signing articles of con-
federation that asserted their unity in matters like defence
and their independence in internal matters. In reality the
union was no more a true federation than the United
Nations or NATO today, for there was no central federal
government; the 'commissioners' from each colony were
primarily advisory. But at least the articles provided some
sort of shield against the outside world—and also gave
the smaller colonies a shield against the rapacity of Massachusetts. Plymouth especially needed one in those days, for
the Bay Colony had been steadily encroaching on its
borders for years.

Rhode Island, which had its application to join the four
bluntly rejected in 1644, found some sort of a shield of its
own when Roger Williams went to England and returned
with a legal charter setting up Rhode Island as a legitimate
colony in its own right. (It was the first official use of the
name—'Rhode' from the Dutch for 'red', referring to soil
colour—and it replaced the older name of Providence
Plantations.) Massachusetts was furious that Puritan England should so favour one of the 'otherwise minded'; but
in fact Williams's personal diplomacy, and his successes
at pacifying the Indians, had won him many plaudits in the
old country, which he used to secure the separate existence
of his colony.

So, in this increasingly uneasy stasis, the New England
colonies settled back, listened to the storm noises in England, and turned inward to attend to North American affairs. The next nearly twenty years of that introversion do
not present the picture that might have been hoped for, of
steady, purposeful and peaceful growth. Of course the individual colonists worked steadily and purposefully, all the
more so given the miniature economic depression that had
struck them, and they made progress in their pioneering.
Edward Johnson, author of a contemporary chronicle of

### Interregnum: Expansion and Oppression

New England entitled *Wonder Working Providence,*
praised those advances:

> The wild and uncouth woods were filled with fre-
> quented ways, and the large rivers were overlaid with
> bridges, passable both for horse and foot.

The southern colonies threw out more and more offspring:
towns like Norwalk and New London (founded with the
help of John Winthrop Jnr) in 'Pequot country', Stamford
and Branford, even towns on Long Island pushing against
Dutch possessions. In Massachusetts new colonial shoots
included Andover, Eastham and Amesbury among many.
And as the pioneers broke new ground and expanded the
colonies, the merchants in Boston and the other larger
coastal towns laid the groundwork for future mercantile
expansion, as when the first Boston-built ship was launched
in the early 1640s, forerunner of a mighty industry. Yet
always, overshadowing all this determined labour and
admirable development, there remained the more typical
New England flavour—of contention and persecution.

Led always by Massachusetts, and in none of these actions
joined by Rhode Island, the colonies meddled in some
French disputes in Acadia (Nova Scotia) to the north, and
emerged discreditably—as they did from their frequent
quarrels, which never quite became a war, with their colonial Dutch neighbours. Equally unpleasantly, the life of the
quasi-federation was marred by continual internecine
squabbles over boundaries and taxes. Massachusetts and
Connecticut quarrelled over who owned Springfield, in
1647; and plentiful murmurings of disapproval arose when
Massachusetts continued its engulfing of the nearer Maine
settlements. In 1653 a new interpretation of the charter's
references to colonial boundaries (see page 45) enabled
Massachusetts to claim land up to three miles north of the
most northerly segment of the Merrimac river. This an-
nexation scooped in several settlements, including Kittery,
whose inhabitants were bluntly told to submit to Bay
Colony rule, unconditionally, or else. By 1658 that rule
had been pushed as far north as Casco Bay, so that all of
settled Maine had become absorbed in Massachusetts—
and would remain so for nearly 200 years.

But the least attractive feature of that inward-looking

period, the 1640s and 1650s, was to be found in the continuing heavy overcast of religious oppression. The banishment
of the Antinomians and the frequent use of the stocks, fines
and imprisonment against divagations from the path all
were harsh enough, but seem trivial by comparison with
later actions. The 1650s brought a new era, when Winthrop, Hooker and Cotton all had died, and when the new
governor was John Endecott, the fanatic who had been a
zealous New Englander since the founding of Salem and
who had shown his ruthlessness in the Pequot war. An important synod of New England churches in the late 1640s
had opened the way for the worst sort of religious persecution, and the first to feel it were a few hapless men from
Rhode Island of a group whose opinions on infant bap-
tism had earned them the name of Baptists.

These men unwisely chose to visit a friend within the
border of Massachusetts, and were summarily arrested, tried
and fined. One of them steadfastly would not acknowledge
the court's right to levy that fine; he was taken out and
flogged, thirty strokes with a three-strand leather whip.
Public opinion, especially among non-Puritans, rose
strongly against this outrage, and news of it even disturbed
New England's friends in the old country. Lord Saltonstall later wrote to Boston expressing his objections, while
during a visit to England John Winthrop's brother Stephen
put his finger on a major cause of the dried-up emigration
to New England: its cruelties in the name of religion
managed to 'discourage any people from coming to us'.

But the theocrats had as it were tasted blood, and would
not be swayed. The next victims guilty of what the synod
had called 'idolatry, blasphemy, heresy, venting corrupt and
pernicious opinions' were a handful of men and women
who proved to be the most significant English emigrants
to New England of the whole Interregnum. They were
Quakers, inflamed and hysterical with the power of their
new spiritual revelation (George Fox had founded the movement in about 1650) and unswervingly determined to hurl
themselves against the Puritan intolerance. If the oligarchy
could have been more flexible, could have allowed them in
and let them perform their antics (as they then were), there
would surely have been few conversions and no serious
threat to the colony. But the rigid policy of exclusion

seemed just as determined as the Quakers themselves to manufacture martyrs.

The first to come to try their hand at converting the Puritans were two women on a ship from the West Indies in 1656. They were arrested, stripped naked and searched, for signs of witchcraft among other possibilities; their books were burned; finally they were imprisoned for eleven weeks, subjected to various other indignities and then put onto a departing ship. In 1657 another group entered Massachusetts, including the remarkable Mary Dyer, a Rhode Island Antinomian who had been converted by a group of Quakers visiting that colony. There they were of course tolerated, and none of Massachusetts' irate letters to Rhode Island leaders altered that reception. As one Rhode Island reply put it,

> freedom of different consciences was the principal
> ground of our charter ... which freedom we still prize
> as the greatest happiness that men can possess in this
> world.

Quakers were also not persecuted in New Amsterdam, and used both these bases to filter into the Bay Colony and the others. Not that it was an infiltration of any size: only about thirty Quakers from England went into Massachusetts, and probably about the same number tried to enter New Haven, Plymouth and Connecticut. (In the latter, it should be noted, they were tolerated almost as well as in Rhode Island.)

By the time Mary Dyer arrived, Massachusetts had passed vicious laws against Quakers, setting out escalating punishments from whipping, through torture with red-hot irons (boring them through tongues was the favourite method) and having ears cut off, up to death by hanging. The worst punishments were reserved for persistent offenders—those who returned after an initial expulsion. So three men of the fifteen who came as a group from New Amsterdam in 1657 were found to be 'recidivists' and lost their right ears; another man was whipped with a rope for so long that the rope gave way, and yet the next day he was whipped ninety-seven more strokes, leaving him with his flesh 'beaten black, and as into a jelly'.

The ordinary people of the Bay Colony grew more and

more distressed at this barbarity, but Endecott and the other leaders ignored public opinion as always. In 1658 they determined to make use of the death penalty if the offences continued; naturally, the Quakers rushed to provide necks for the ropes. Mary Dyer and two men were arrested and sentenced to die, but only the men were hanged, while Mary was merely banished. Insistently, she returned in 1660, and forced the Puritan fanaticism to give her the martyrdom she wished. But when Mary was hanged the public fury became so audible that even Endecott took notice; and though one more Quaker was to be hanged, in 1661, the authorities drew back to their earlier position when punishments were merely torture and flogging. So, for instance, in 1662 three Quaker women were stripped to the waist in deep winter, tied behind carts and whipped ten lashes in each of eleven Massachusetts towns as the carts dragged them through and out of the colony.

By then, however, the opposition to even these punishments from within the colonies had acquired a powerful new ally—the newly restored Charles II, whose mere presence on the throne had created an earthquake that severely damaged the theocracy's secure position. Charles was clearly going to look very closely at developments in America's stronghold of Puritanism; indeed, soon after Mary Dyer's execution the new king had sent strongly worded messages telling the Massachusetts leaders to kill no more Quakers, and stressing that the laws of *England* were the only laws operating in English colonies. And shortly afterwards, the death of Endecott also helped to weaken the forces of fanaticism in the colonial leadership.

The broad view of history indicates that the general, overall climate during the Restoration period and on to the civilized heights of the eighteenth century was freshened by many breezes of liberalization and reform, as by many other wide-ranging sorts of change and reappraisal. New England would be affected and altered by this progress in many ways—as the mother country sought to re-establish closer links, not to say controls; as a second generation of colonists, New England-born, took charge of the colonists' destiny; as the political and economic stature of the colonies, in international terms, began to enlarge and mature.

Yet for decades, such was the strength of the old estab-

*The determined Quaker, Mary Dyer, being escorted to her execution*

lished binding theocratic ways, life in New England would seem to change only subtly and marginally, the intrusions of the new century seeping in only gradually. Day by day, as New England life was lived, it would seem that the old restrictions and oppressions rode as securely as ever on the colonists' backs.

# 5. Eighteenth Century: Alarums and Excursions

Any observer then or now could be forgiven for expecting the newly restored king of England to impose himself crushingly on the colonial Puritans, as he had on the English Puritans in their post-Cromwell disarray. Certainly Charles II had no reason to love New England. The colonies had clearly taken upon themselves all manner of sovereign rights as if they were independent states. Their fast-growing mercantilism was offering potentially painful competition to English foreign trade. They defied English law by cruelly persecuting other religious sects. And, the ultimate insult, they provided sanctuary in 1660 for William Goffe and Edward Whalley, two of Cromwell's men who had signed Charles I's death warrant, and who were pursued by royalist officers to Boston, then to a haven in New Haven, finally to a successful disappearance in the wilderness of New Hampshire's frontier.

But kings and politicians are unpredictable, and will forgo revenge if advantage can otherwise be gained. All the New England colonies hurried to turn Charles's wrath by formally proclaiming his restoration—Rhode Island and Connecticut first, New Haven grudgingly last—and in response he proved generous. Rhode Island and Connecticut sent John Winthrop Jnr to London as their emissary, and he exerted all his diplomacy (with not a little bribery) to obtain for them the security of full royal charters. Indeed, Connecticut delightedly found itself defined as a much larger area than it had hoped—and this liberality of the charter meant that it engulfed New Haven, which, its protests ignored, had to submit to this loss of individuality. Some tension arose when a segment of the Narragansett lands looked like being lost by Rhode Island to Connecticut; but in the main the new charters allowed these

# THE

# CHARTER

### Granted by His MAJESTY

### King CHARLES

## The SECOND,

## TO THE

# COLONY

## OF

# Rhode-Island,

## AND

## Providence Plantations,

## In AMERICA.

*NEWPORT, Rhode-Island:*
Printed by JAMES FRANKLIN, and Sold at his Shop near
the Town School-House, 1730.

*The title-page of the charter granted to Rhode Island in 1730*

two least repressive and most forward-looking colonies to continue on their self-contained ways. Connecticut's charter, indeed, was so liberal that it provided the basic constitutional framework of the *state* until the 1840s.

In Massachusetts, where the old restrictive Puritan order was gradually giving way to the bright, bold, mercantile new, the existing charter was perfunctorily confirmed. But at the same time the king decided to have the place investigated, in the light of past complaints against it. These included the continuing rage of Gorges' and Mason's heirs, over Massachusetts' takeover of the Maine and New Hampshire settlements. The king also decided to use the investigation to cloak the buildup of a military action—which would involve New England fighting men—against the Dutch holdings in America. Out, then, went a Royal Commission in 1664, helped in the nearly effortless victory over the Dutch that made New York English, looked at Connecticut, Rhode Island and Plymouth and pronounced them good. The commissioners especially gushed over Rhode Island with its 'best English grass and most sheep, the ground very fruitful...' while the frontier towns on the Piscataqua were praised for their industriousness, having 'twenty sawmills' that turned out masts as well as lumber. The sad decline of Plymouth was reflected in the commission's note on its lack of development: 'one sawmill for boards, one bloomery for iron, neither good river nor good harbour, nor any place of strength'.

As for Massachusetts, while its capital seemed made mainly of rude wooden houses on crooked streets 'with little decency and no uniformity', at least Harvard College had arisen at Cambridge to take care of intellectual matters while the busy, thriving merchants of the towns took care of commercial ones. The commission noted with approval the booming trade in

> fish, which was sent into France, Spain and the Straits, pipe-staves, masts, fir boards, some pitch and tar, pork, beef, horses, and corn, which they sent to Virginia, Barbadoes, etc., and took tobacco and sugar in payment. . . .

But these were exterior matters. When the commissioners tried to penetrate into the workings of the colonial ad-

ministration, the power structure and so on, they ran
sharply into the obstructionist, delaying tactics aptly called
'stone-walling' in American slang. No one co-operated,
records seemed unavailable, rumours discrediting the Commissioners were put about, and more. Though the Commission eventually recommended that Massachusetts' days
of theocracy and autonomy be ended, the delaying techniques worked, once again—when as before (and the oligarchy still called it providence) England and the king
had too many other things to worry about at home: plague,
the fire of London, war and parliamentary upheaval.

Massachusetts was not, however, to breathe easily for
long. Another investigation was due to be made within a
few years—and by then New England would have had its
own home-grown crisis to focus its attention. It was largely
of the colonies' own making, due to their continual expansion into the back country, which meant more and more
pressure put on the Indian tribes who happened to occupy
those regions. In any case the tribes had no love for Puritans who reacted to 'heathen' Indians with condescension
at best, repressive laws and physical mistreatment at worst.
Nor could extensive work by missionaries, producing some
4,000 'praying-Indian' converts, counteract the effect of
the more typical colonial attitudes; and besides, the uncon-
verted Indians resented the missionaries' paternalist presence as much as the settlers'. Anger that had been building
up since the Pequot War merely awaited the striking of a
spark: the chief called 'King Philip' provided it.

He was the son of Massasoit, to whom the Pilgrims owed
so much: yet the Plymouth colonists felt no compunction
when in 1671 they imposed severe humiliations on Philip
for 'plotting' against the colony. Philip, whose majesty was
never particularly serene, was afterwards plotting his revenge when events overtook him. Sporadic Indian raids, not
ordered or controlled by Philip, had begun to occur all
along the frontier: tribes other than Philip's, including
the Narragansetts, began to take part, and soon these
separate flash fires grew together to become one vast blaz-
ing front around New England. What had been raids became, by 1675, mass assaults with Philip opportunistically
at the head of a loose tribal alliance. Frontier towns were
evacuated, and colonial militia tramped back and forth
seeking the enemy, which usually proved elusive to the

point of invisibility, as when they evaded a force from Springfield and slipped in behind it to burn the town.

The Indians might well have won this first major Indian uprising of the north-east, except that the Puritan forces were in the long run better armed, better supplied and more unified of purpose than the tribes. The winter proved disastrous to King Philip's plans, when the food supplies dwindled to nothing and the tribes began squabbling as various chiefs tried to dislodge Philip as supreme commander. Eventually starvation and a lucky shot that killed Philip brought the war to an end in the spring of 1676. But the victory had not been gained without leaving terrible scars on the colonies. About 500 men had been lost (one-tenth of the adult men of Massachusetts were killed), about twenty villages partly or wholly destroyed, about £100,000 of badly needed colonial money spent. At that point, still worn from Indian fighting, the colonists had little life left to counter a new challenge from England.

In the old country in 1675 the king had set up a committee called the Lords of Trade, precursors of today's Board of Trade; and like all new brooms it had gone determinedly into action, especially examining all colonies that might be getting above themselves. In 1676 they sent one Edward Randolph to scrutinize Massachusetts. Randolph, a man of some ambition, nosed and probed and finally reported extensive flouting of English law generally and trade restrictions in particular, and a widespread attitude of insufficient loyalty and subservience to royal authority. All these things were, of course, true. When the Lords demanded explanations from Massachusetts, the colony began another of those previously effective delaying actions. But this time, while developments were somewhat slowed and hindered, no new providence arrived to divert official attention and save the colony.

The Lords of Trade took action in 1679, ordering that New Hampshire should be separated from Massachusetts, to become a crown colony. Then it took further action, upon receiving messages of astonishingly arrogant, and suicidal, defiance from the Massachusetts oligarchy. After some legal entanglement the order went through in 1684 for the *revocation* of the Massachusetts charter, so it, too, could be brought under royal control. Providence almost rescued the colony when Charles II died the following year;

but James II agreed to the revocation, and also to the grander plan that had emerged. The Lords of Trade sought strength (against the French, among other things, but also against internal subversion) in unity, and decided to unite the New England colonies. Once action had also been taken against the Connecticut and Rhode Island charters (Plymouth, remember, had never had a charter, only a shaky proprietary patent) the 'Dominion of New England' was born. This birth, of course, put a final end to the old federation, the 'United Colonies'—but with the defeat of the Dutch colonies and the later victory over the Indians, much of the original motive force (of mutual security) behind the federation had dissipated. And, given the usual intercolony quarrels and suspicion, their self-created union had since 1675 been allowed tacitly to become defunct. Now it was officially dead and buried, and in its place stood a true union—and a larger one. The new dominion encompassed Massachusetts, Connecticut, Plymouth, Rhode Island, Maine, New Hampshire and also the newer colonies of New York and New Jersey. In 1686 Sir Edmund Andros arrived at Boston to fill the role of first royal governor of Britain's American possessions.

He filled it badly. He flung the Church of England into Puritan faces; he enforced stringently the laws against colonies trading directly with foreign nations or importing foreign goods directly; he brought in British troops; he imposed harsh taxes; he even threatened the old land grant system that might have questioned long-held titles to land in the colonies. It may well have been that, in time, the colonists would have risen against him. But instead (was it that providence again, if belated?) the rising was performed for them, in England. The landing of William of Orange in 1688 and shortly the accession of William and Mary to the English throne gave New England their chance: Andros was deposed and arrested, and a provisional government took over. Nowhere, perhaps, was that Revolution felt to be more Glorious.

In England then, the eminent Puritan divine, Increase Mather, sought a renewal of Massachusetts' charter. With the new regime he was ultimately successful, but the charter of 1691 turned out to be a compromise, not at all what Mather and the old theocracy wanted. The colony was to retain an English governor, was to have an extended franchise *not* dependent on church membership, and would insist upon religious toleration. At the same time the colony could be pleased by the new extension of its area, which gave official sanction to its absorption of Maine. Also the new boundaries ordained that Massachusetts should at last swallow up Plymouth, putting an end to that separation of the first New England colony which was so greatly prized by its first separatist residents. New Hampshire continued as a royal colony, Connecticut and Rhode Island had their former charters restored, and all seemed set fair for New England to sail into the eighteenth century with a certain amount of peace and security.

But such commodities were hard to come by anywhere, and certainly in New England. Puritan rigour had what may be called one last burst of strength in the early 1690s, when the irresponsible and hysterical actions of some young girls in the back country near Salem led to a colony-wide panic that resulted in the inquisitorial trials of hundreds and the barbarous execution of at least twenty, all suspected of 'witchcraft'. On the threshold of the age that would be called the 'Enlightenment', Massachusetts slipped back into the frenzied state that Europe had known during its fifteenth- and sixteenth-century witch persecutions.

It may be true that the aftermath of the hysteria, rich in guilt and anti-Puritan backlash, served as much as the new political structure to pry loose whatever remained of the old theocratic grip on the colony. In any case, as the new century began, New England turned with a will, and with few voices decrying it, to outright commercialism and mercantilism, in the true English empire-building mould. The eighteenth century may have been a time for a tremendous explosion in fairly peaceful pursuits like science and technology, literature and philosophy, the arts and the crafts. But it was also an age of a mighty expansion of foreign trade, a build-up of Britannia's potential wave-ruling—and all the flare-ups of international violence that such growth seemed to carry with it. New England, embracing the growth, partook also of the wars. The restored Stuarts had fought Holland, and New England had dutifully invested New Amsterdam. Now William and Mary directed their military adventurings at the main threat to England's fast-rising fortunes, the France of Louis XIV. England was to be fighting France off and on for more than

100 years; her North American possessions were in every case drawn into the fray.

A negotiated peace in Europe in 1697 saved New England from disaster at the hands of the redoubtable Frontenac of New France (Canada) in the first collision, called King William's War. Afterwards the French of the St Lawrence and Acadia pushed more often and harder against the vulnerable New England frontier; and when the War of the Spanish Succession broke out in 1703, French assaults nearly broke through and overran that frontier—except that England sent troops and saved the day. Then the assaults were reversed, and New England helped in the successful overrunning of Acadia—which, by the Treaty of Utrecht in 1713, was given into English hands. But by then those hands were British, not merely English, and Acadia became Nova Scotia, eventually to be one of several major North American havens for disaffected and emigrant Scots.

The period that began after 1713, and up to 1760, may have known prosperity from booming trade, and may have seen Georgian ideas of order, balance, comfort and civilization take hold in every aspect of life, whether architecture, finance, furniture design, government, poetry or theology. Of course that portrait is idealized, ignoring a multitude of warts. There was no shortage of wars to disturb that Augustan peace, as when the conflict over Jenkins' Ear erupted in 1739. And for a truer picture of Georgian prosperity and security one might have asked a farm labourer —or, perhaps more usefully here, some of the many thousands who turned their backs on England's Enlightenment to seek some sort of fortune in the uncivilized colonies. After 1713 there was a tidal outpouring of people to America that made the Puritan migration a century before seem trivial by comparison.

As it happened, very few of these eighteenth-century emigrants went to New England, as is indicated by the result of a query sent out to the colonies by the English government in 1680, asking each: 'What number of English, Scotch and Irish foreigners [sic] have, during the past seven years . . . come yearly to plant and inhabit within your corporation . . .?' And Connecticut, for one, replied:

for English, Scotch and Irish, there are so few come

in that we cannot give a certain account: some years come none; sometimes a family or two in a year.

The reasons for this refusal are instructive. One of them, though not merely affecting New England, was official British policy. A notion had become more and more widespread that emigration—to anywhere—was a dangerous drain of one of a nation's primary resources, its population: mercantilism still dictated that colonies were principally suppliers of cheap raw materials and markets for finished goods—not yet dumping grounds for surplus people. Abundant population at home, it was felt, ensured abundant cannon fodder in wartime, cheap labour in peace. And at all costs, the cream of the nation's labour, the skilled crafstman or artisan, must be kept at home: in the eighteenth century their emigration was forbidden by law. (And later, when America began making revolutionary noises, George III would try to clamp down on all emigration to those colonies.)

More importantly, New England had managed thoroughly to blacken its image in the British mind over the decades—and such features of the colony as the growing scarcity of unoccupied fertile land, the frontier presence of hostile Indians, the malevolent winters, needed no extra blackening. But New England was also the place where Puritans had exercised their rigid intolerance, their stifling theocracy, their brutal persecutions of Quakers, Baptists and others, so that as noted in Chapter 4 even the Puritan Lord Saltonstall had begun diverting emigrants to the West Indies.

And here of course was a central reason why few went to New England: there were so many other places to go. America was full of colonies—Pennsylvania and the Delaware developments, Maryland, Virginia, the splendid new Carolinas, soon Georgia. Who then would seek the bleak Puritan shores of Massachusetts with such alternatives? Certainly not the Quakers, who poured across the Atlantic in the wake of William Penn, before the turn of the century, but of whom only a tiny minority braved New England's suspicion. A few thousand refugee Huguenots from France decided for New England before 1700, but faced a good deal of mistreatment (in Rhode Island and Connecticut especially) and most moved on to New York or the Carolinas. And nearly 100,000 German-speaking people, generally Protestant and mostly fleeing the French assaults on the Rhineland, ignored New England and chose instead the warmer welcomes of Pennsylvania.

The bulk of Britain's contribution to this new 'great migration' came from the Celtic fringe. Assorted Scotsmen began to filter across the Atlantic, including a fair number of embittered Catholic Highlanders after the failures of their two eighteenth-century risings in 1715 and 1745. But while no doubt a few Lowlanders may have made their way into New England, most Highland emigrants preferred the backwoods of upper New York state, or the Carolinas. And they would be, until after the Revolution, vastly fewer in number than the emigrant descendants of those Protestant Scots planted in Northern Ireland by James I, a century or more before.

These 'Scotch-Irish', as the American colonists insisted on calling emigrants from Ulster, thronged into the colonies in ever-increasing numbers: one estimate states that a quarter of a million Ulstermen migrated during the first seventy years of the century. They left to escape crushing restrictions on their trade with Britain, that undermined all their determined attempts to boost the Ulster economy; they left because of severe discrimination against their Presbyterian religion; they left because of a sequence of droughts and pathetic crops; they left because absentee landlords had heaped intolerable rent rises onto all these other hardships. About five thousand of the emigrants had anticipated better lives in New England, but found an unexpected barrier of religious intolerance in their way. (The New England Puritans were Calvinists of the 'Congregational' type, so that Presbyterianism seemed doctrinally as distasteful to them as Quaker or Baptist beliefs.) Many of the Ulster emigrants eventually drifted off into more tolerant Pennsylvania, where direct emigration had previously planted several groups of their compatriots. But others determined to stay—out on the rugged and wild frontiers of New Hampshire and Maine where they built their main settlement, Londonderry. There they found their fierce, violent Northern Irish ways of considerable value: they made names for themselves as prodigious Indian fighters, and also (if anyone had listened) as a seething hotbed of hatred for English authority.

## Eighteenth Century: Alarums and Excursions

Yet in among all these waves of other emigrants there were some few English folk throughout the eighteenth century who chose to emigrate, and who chose New England—where one mid-century estimate said that only 5 per cent of the population was *not* of English descent. They may have been only a handful, a few hundred perhaps—but when they came (most noticeably in the 1720s) they had a considerable effect, especially on Boston. That city's commercial growth attracted them, according to C. K. Shipton in his account of this small but noticeable emigration; and their arrival, swelling the ranks of the merchants and shopkeepers and the like, helped to make Boston a more fully commercial centre—as Shipton says, erasing further 'the Puritan peculiarities of the town, and of the upper class of New Englander in general'. He adds that, obviously, the majority of these English emigrants would have been shopkeepers, 'small capitalists', and a fair number of artisans who had slipped through the net of the law against their departure. There was also a constant sprinkling of deserters, either drifting down from Acadia and Newfoundland or fleeing from ships in Boston harbour (one ship in 1720 lost twenty-six seamen at once).

And up to the 1720s many of the newcomers would have been indentured servants, bound to a temporary servitude to whomever owned their bond, and therefore saleable like cattle—or slaves. A brisk trade in 'bondsmen' lasted for some years, mainly based in Bristol, whereby ships brought indentured workers to be sold to labour-hungry colonists at considerable profit. At one time in Boston in 1717 six entire shiploads of indentured servants stood awaiting sale. Many such indentured servants are noted in E. S. Bolton's laconic catalogue of emigrants to New England before 1775, among them Jonathan Hartley from Yorkshire, who arrived in 1699 with seven years to serve—at the age of eighteen; or Jane Radcliff from Lancashire, unmarried twenty-year-old also with seven years to serve. (It is possible, though, that these two were convicts, since a seven-year sentence to the colonies came to be fairly commonplace as a substitute for other punishments at home.) But later the trade declined, partly as the market was glutted, partly because some colonists preferred black slaves from Africa, partly because English bondsmen had the annoying habit of running away, or dying, before their terms were up.

E. S. Bolton's list—which of course makes no pretence at being complete—offers some other tantalizing allusive glimpses of eighteenth-century English emigrants. There were, naturally, an inordinate number of clergymen—including a brave Church of England minister named Matthias Plant, who arrived in Newbury, Mass., before 1722. There was the whole family of Saunders—patriarch, four sons, their wives and families—from Torbay, who settled on the 'Isles of Shoals' in New Hampshire, at mid-century. There was a multitude of fortunate artisans— ironmongers, butchers, sailmakers, ropemakers, cordwainers, cutlers, physicians, feltmakers, spectacle makers, hosts of tailors, and a Mrs E. Atkinson travelling alone to Boston in 1729 who was a dressmaker. There was Thomas Attwood, 'gent.', from Bristol to Boston in 1716, and R. Chandler, a London gentleman, in the same year. There were abundant 'husbandmen' seeking to better themselves; there were disaffected seamen looking for the ultimate landfall. There was one John Waghorne who arrived in Boston before 1739 professing to teach 'japanning' and 'vocal Psalmody'. And there was the admirable Joseph Cates, who left Greenwich for the rugged frontier joys of Gorham, Maine, before 1745, and who fathered ten children in New England and died at the age of eighty-nine.

But even this fairly inconsequential English emigration dwindled almost to vanishing point after mid-century. According to an important article by Mildred Campbell, in the years before the American Revolution about 6,000 emigrant departures for America were recorded (but records were by no means widely or well kept) from London, Yorkshire, the West Country and other regions. Of these people only fifty-six took passage for New England. Others would have been deterred, in part, when Boston's boom times sagged a little with stiff competition from other colonial capitals like New York or Baltimore, and when war in Europe meant war in America—which in turn meant the threat of the French and their Iroquois allies on the northern colonial frontier. The Seven Years' War may have put New England's economy onto a wartime footing, but it also meant a series of dangerous defeats for the colonies when the conflict spread to the backwoods. Eventually, however, as most North American schoolchildren will know, British forces carried the war to the enemy: the 'impregnable' fort of Louisbourg fell, Wolfe sent his Highland troops over the cliffs to win on the Plains of Abraham, and Britain gained the ownership of Canada. That victory was of course to mean a new source of competition for the few straggling British emigrants of the 1760s and 1770s. But at least New England had gained a more secure northwest frontier—even if by then the general security and peace of the colonies was being undermined by the last threat they would ever face, as colonies.

The radical political undercurrents building at this time are only obliquely relevant to the subject of emigration, primarily because they served in some measure to inhibit it. But if anyone needs a brief recapitulation, it might be enough to note British attempts at tightening imperial controls over self-interested colonies when Lord Halifax took over the Board of Trade in 1748, the further attempts when Pitt became Prime Minister in 1758, and the ultimately crucial attempts when George III mounted the throne in 1760. These men were not aiming their efforts solely at recalcitrant colonies who would insist on governing themselves, but at freewheeling mercantilist colonies competing with British trade in Europe, the West Indies and elsewhere, often in the face of legalized restrictions—and sometimes even discovered to be trading with the colonial possessions of the French enemy, during wartime. So grievance piled upon grievance, defiance upon defiance; though the process was diverted somewhat by the fearful uprising in 1763 of Pontiac's Ottawa Indians on the northern frontier, the colonies were rushing towards a final rejection of the mother country.

Postwar economic cutbacks brought heavy taxes from Britain, and more restrictions and duties to affect New England trade. Later in the 1760s the notorious Stamp Act, desperately costly for the colonies, aroused more defiance, which in turn stiffened Britain's intentions to impose its authority on America. As the confrontation hardened, British troops were moved about in the colonies, especially towards Boston—and there, in 1770, after weeks of simmering animosity, a mob attacked a detachment of those troops and were fired upon. The five colonists who died were immortalized as the 'Boston Massacre', and the progress

*The Boston Massacre, as seen, engraved and perhaps over-dramatized by Paul Revere, who was a printer among other things before his famous ride*

towards collision gathered speed. Boston held its history-making tea party, Britain countered by closing the port of Boston, and soon afterwards infuriated every Anglo-Saxon Protestant colonist by the (actually quite laudable) Quebec Act that demanded toleration of Catholicism in Canada and that pushed the borders of that colony down into the fur-rich forests of Ohio, wrenching them out of American hands.

It was not long before some very important colonial leaders were gathered in America's first meeting of Congress, while others abandoned debate for the barricades at Lexington and Concord, Massachusetts. The shots fired there may not have truly been, in Emerson's grandiose phrase, 'heard round the world'. But they ensured that any English emigrants to New England from then on would be going to a foreign country.

# 6. Second Colonization

When that famous dawn's early light finally illuminated the end of the American War of Independence, New England was not altered out of all recognition. But it would be, comparatively soon. The seeds or first shoots of major change, which have been noted before—in such developments as the mercantilist outburst, the decline of theocratic repression and corresponding hints of liberalization, the influx of other nationalities—all now found a chance to sprout more rapidly than ever. New England life and character, which had been fixed in the early seventeenth century and had been maintained in a near-stasis well into the eighteenth, began to undergo a massive transition.

The destruction in the ex-colonies wreaked by the revolution itself might have been worse: most of the major land battles occurred in other regions, and the worst dislocations in New England arose from naval raids, the British occupation of Rhode Island, and temporary evacuations of Boston and other centres and the absence of men from their homes to fight in the militia. Economically, of course, all the thirteen states had suffered in those violent birth throes—as the ragged and starving state of Washington's troops had attested—from scarcities and rocketing prices, aided in no small measure by some merchants' blatant profiteering. But at the same time there were less anti-social ways to gain the wealth that is always to be gained by some in wartime. Many New Englanders made solid fortunes through some enterprising privateering—which is, of course, the form of piracy that has a quasi-legal backing. Most significantly for the future, some towns had previously launched themselves in small ways into manufacturing, and found the war to be excellent growing ground for their embryonic industries. The town of Lynn, for instance, made

money making shoes, Springfield expanded its metal industry by making arms, some Rhode Island towns took up
nail-making.

Such developments away from the conventional emphasis
in the colonies on agriculture were clear hints of things to
come—and so, too, was a further relaxation (not to say
laxity) in some of the old social mores and requirements.
New England would never lose some sense of social hier-
archy, left from the old seventeenth-century oligarchic structure, but during and after the Revolution class mobility
proved easier, especially when *nouveaux riches* sprouted
everywhere. And because the dislocation of war pried even
looser the grip on society of the religious establishment, the
social one naturally loosened as well. But equally significant was the *actual* mobility of New Englanders—not up
through the social strata but out of New England.

Such departures had been going on almost from the
beginning, as has been seen; and in the mid-eighteenth
century, with New England's good land mostly filled up,
New Englanders had ranged far—south to the Carolinas
and Georgia, a few brave souls over the mountains into the
western wilderness, many northwards into what remained of
unsettled frontier Maine and New Hampshire. Of settlers
in the latter, land-hungry as always, some had pushed well
beyond the Connecticut river to take up wild land granted
to them by New Hampshire. Settlement continued sporadic-
ally on these 'New Hampshire Grants' before and during
the war, in the teeth of claims from New York that the
lands were not New Hampshire's to grant.

The residents of this frontier region, who had multiplied
to about 30,000 by the end of the Revolution, resisted New
York's claims. When the latter grew forceful, some leading
frontiersmen in the Grants including Ethan Allen and his
brothers quickly built up a fighting force glamorously
called the 'Green Mountain Boys', and prepared to wage
their own private war of independence. It never came to
that: but the willingness, if the need arose, contributed to
the spirit that in 1777 declared the New Hampshire Grants
to be the separate and sovereign nation of Vermont. (The
name was obviously derived from 'green mountain', after
a flirtation with the idea of calling it New Connecticut—
an indication of the main source of the population flow
that had created it.)

Vermont briefly courted the British in an effort to achieve recognition and some security, but with little result save to create suspicion throughout the rest of New England. Meanwhile during the war and in the years that followed, typical internecine wrangling went on over the Vermont boundaries. But then the new states were always squabbling over their borders: Connecticut and Pennsylvania had actually gone to war against each other in the midst of the Revolution. Similar quarrels and struggles, and corollary difficulties over forming state governments and agreeing on constitutions, occupied much energy long after the peace had been signed in 1783.

These political factors provided an extra element in the postwar insecurities that disturbed New England in the 1780s—but the worst of these were of course economic. Peace meant an end of profitable privateering and arms manufacture and the like. Peace also meant the need to expand foreign trade—but Britain was crushingly imposing restrictions on trade with her colonies, causing the young United States in some pique to impose its own counter-restrictions, in the familiar tradition of nose-cutting and face-spiting. A financial crisis of some desperation resulted, deepened by abundant get-rich-quick speculation—which eventually drove rioters out into the streets demanding state intervention in the out-of-control economy.

All such developments served naturally to spur on the emigration out of New England, now more and more looking past even the frontiers of Maine and Vermont towards the inviting (because more fertile) emptiness of upper New York, Pennsylvania beyond the Allegheny mountains and farther still to wildest Ohio. Now not occasional hardy frontiersmen but a steady flow of pioneer families were at last over-running the Appalachians, of which the Alleghenies were one range, which had for so long been a natural barrier against any free and easy westward movement by New Englanders. These departures, in their tens of thousands, were paralleled by the more hasty exodus of Empire Loyalists, also in their thousands, who fled persecution or its threat and went north to take up life again under the British flag, thereby also transforming the Canadian colonies. The spaces they left behind, the relief their absence provided within the New England population pressures, created ideal circumstances for the build-up of a new flow of emigration from the Old World that would, in New England, come to be thought of as a 'second colonization'.

In other areas the new arrivals had already passed through the build-up stage and were in full flood: from 1783 to the next major historical turning point, 1815, about a quarter of a million emigrants of various nationalities landed at American ports. But hardly more than an edge of this wave touched New England. Indeed, those states appeared to be in something of a decline in relative importance within the Union. By 1790 New Englanders numbered only about 25 per cent of the nation's population where a century before they had been 50 per cent. And the ultimate decision of Vermont's 85,000 people to become the fourteenth state, and New England's fifth, in 1791 provided only a few more drops in an emptying bucket. While New York, Philadelphia, even Baltimore burst with population, post-revolution Boston sagged and stagnated, watching its people and much of its trade drain off to the thriving 'middle states'.

There, too, went the bulk of the postwar immigrants— more Ulster Irish, about 20,000 in the first decade of American independence; more Germans, including some 5,000 mercenaries who stayed as settlers after the war; more indentured servants of every sort, until new laws dictating how many people could be jammed onto a ship undercut the profits in that trade. French royalist refugees arrived in flight from the Revolution, followed later by revolutionaries in flight from the Terror. Numerous Irish Catholic rebels came after 1798, to escape retaliation after the rising of that year. And also the newborn 'land of the free' attracted a good many Britons who leaned towards radical, reformist, democratic attitudes and who suffered in the conservative backlash that followed the declaration of war with revolutionary France in 1793. Notable among these radicals was Joseph Priestley, scientist and reformer, who had barely escaped harm in the notorious Birmingham riots.

But the more ordinary Europeans who entered America did so not as refugees from revolutions or idealists seeking Utopia but as willing hopefuls who had succumbed to the swelling chorus of propaganda making it clear that the land of the free was also the land of opportunity. Priestley

himself added to it, with his widely publicized description
of life in Pennsylvania in 1796:

> Here we have no poor; we never see a beggar, nor is
> there a family in want. We have no church establish-
> ment, and hardly any taxes....

In this he, like others, echoed the pæan of that notable
French emigrant, de Crèvecoeur, who wrote eloquently of
the possibilities open to everyone, whatever his trade or pro-
fession, and added:

> I do not mean that every one who comes will grow
> rich in a little time; no, but he may procure an easy,
> decent maintenance by his industry. Instead of starv-
> ing, he will be fed; instead of being idle, he will have
> employment; and these are riches enough for such
> men as come over here. The rich stay in Europe, it is
> only the middling and the poor that emigrate.

Certainly New England experienced some benefit from
such propaganda, even though by far the bulk of the
current emigration passed it by. But what small share those
states did receive turned out to be of special importance in
the long run with regard to the manufacturing industry—
which, as noted, was embryonic during the Revolution and
which remained in its infancy during the 1780s and 1790s
(and more or less retarded, too, by generally stunted economic growth). All the same, a good few Englishmen and
Scotsmen had begun to appear in the mills that did exist,
as when a number of deserters and leftovers from the
British army stayed on and helped to set up the first stages
of woollen mills in Hartford. The skills of such men were
increasingly at a premium, as New England developed its
far-reaching changeover to manufacturing—to a great extent because the expansion of its agriculture had clear
limits, in terms of fertility and population, and these
seemed to have been reached in the 1790s. But such skills
were not easily obtained. England still had its old laws
against the emigration of 'artisans'—and against the re-
moval from the country of industrial machinery or even
drawings of machinery. It was clear that the old country
was, sensibly, not going to give any aid or encouragement

to a potential competitor already well known for high-powered trading methods.

Yet as always before, the artisans and skilled workers who were determined to cross the Atlantic got round the law—some by posing as agricultural labourers, others by emigrating to Canada, which, as part of the Empire, was not covered by the law, and slipping across the unguarded border into America. And their presence hastened the transition in New England from farming and cottage industries to full industrialization. One of the most famous of such arrivals was that of Samuel Slater, an English workman who memorized drawings of the latest variants on Arkwright's spinning jenny and made his way to Rhode Island, where his priceless knowledge led to the creation in 1793 of a successful cotton mill—America's first. (Thereby Slater became the country's first industrial spy.) In that year, too, John and Arthur Scholfield came from Yorkshire with their heads full of technology and built the machines for new mills in various Massachusetts towns that vastly advanced the New England woollen industry.

The fact of the French wars in Europe at this time did not wholly inhibit emigration, though no doubt without the hostilities that quarter of a million before 1815 would have been a much larger figure. Certainly many wisely stayed off the seas to avoid the two opposing evils—attack by French privateers, or boarding by British press gangs ever hungry for extra hands for the expanding Navy. And when after a brief breathing space the Anglo-French conflict resumed as the Napoleonic wars, in 1803, with the British blockade of Europe and so on, emigration to America from anywhere died away. Any small driblets that might have continued were then blocked finally by the growing hostility of the United States towards its former masters—a hostility provoked considerably by high-handed British actions at sea—which eventually led to the outbreak of the War of 1812.

That rather bungled conflict, which served mainly to stimulate Canadian unity and national feeling when those tiny colonies threw back an American invasion, came to an end with the general cessation of battle round the world. So the unfamiliarity of peace settled on to Europe in 1815, and brought chaos with it. From the standpoint of emigration, the more important elements of that chaos seem to

have been the appalling unemployment and displacement
that was occurring with the industrial revolution, and the
agricultural, worsened by the demobilization and return
home of thousands of soldiers. Also, national economies
were shifting down into peacetime gears, and the forces of
radicalism and conservatism were continuing to jostle for
dominance—all exacerbating the shattering upheavals of
those changing times.

But of course the old 'push-pull' view of emigration and
its causes must once more be stressed: people did not in-
evitably leave to escape upheaval, but often simply because
the fact of upheaval made it possible for them to consider
leaving—the undermining of the old fixed social order,
tradition and convention, showing people that they could
after all hope for better. So one way or another the unrest
and turmoil, economic or otherwise, promoted emigration
which in some measure promoted more unrest and turmoil.
Perhaps it all shows the hopelessness of analysing 'causes'
of immense and widespread mass migration, as if they were
viruses that one might isolate under a microscope. The
nineteenth-century emigration fever may have been an infection, but its causal agents and recognizable symptoms
were legion—and each nation, each shipload, each individual put those elements together in his or her or its own
proportions.

Up to about 1825, the various states of the Union concerned themselves busily with tidying up after war and
with their own versions of political and economic upheaval. They could not have guessed that millions upon
millions of people stood poised, as it were, to come 'crowd-
ing in on ships from all corners of the world to the great
gates of North America', in Emerson's words. New Englanders were more preoccupied with their own continuing
emigration, as Yankee families continued to stream over
the mountains into the west—pushing in among earlier
pioneers in Indiana and Illinois, or after 1825 moving into
the unpopulated wilds even farther to the north-west to
impose the New England flavour on the frontiers of
Michigan and Wisconsin. As this voluminous population
drain continued, New Englanders at home went on trying
to adjust themselves to the new century—injecting more
true democracy into their state governments, improving
upon their state constitutions in the light of the newly

ratified federal Constitution and so on. In some states, though religious leaders who still clung to the remnants of Puritanism foamed at the mouth, the new constitutions officially recognized the now limited role of the church, as when Connecticut legislated for the formal separation of church and state and for equal rights for all denominations.

In Massachusetts, political furore arose over the voluble demands for separation from the 300,000 people who lived in Maine. Any previous stirrings of national feeling in Maine since its absorption in 1658 had come to nothing when the region's population was small and scattered: so the 'absentee government' in Boston had been able to maintain control of the northern towns and that valuable harbour-strewn coastline. But now the pressure from Maine proved harder to resist, especially when the blatant old land-grabbing and repressive Massachusetts methods were so increasingly in disrepute. In the end Massachusetts could find no way to hinder Maine from extricating itself, and in 1820 Maine became New England's sixth and last state.

If high points like the westward expansion and the birth of Maine, as well as the increasingly controversial issue of slavery, which is somewhat outside the scope of this narrative, did not sufficiently occupy New England's attention, its own rapid industrial revolution provided another matter of major concern. More and more merchants who had once put their investment capital into shipping were turning to manufacturing, which blossomed further when post-war tariffs went up to protect home-made goods. Textiles advanced fastest—wool mills in Connecticut, cotton in Massachusetts and Rhode Island—with dozens of new firms springing up every year after 1815. Recessions and financial panics, especially that of 1819, now and then inhibited the speed of the industrializing process, but only temporarily. As the mills and factories multiplied and spread, as the urbanization that is the corollary to industrialization further depleted the villages and swelled the cities, the first ripples of the immense mid-century movement of Europeans to America began to lap the shores of New England.

Figures were generally incomplete then, and give an inadequate picture now. Even so, it is worth noting in pass-

ing that those ripples remained small for many years after
the great slump of 1819: one estimate says that only 1,400
people came in through New England ports as late as 1825.
To some extent the laws restricting the departure of skilled
workers still acted as a partial dam, while farmers and
other labourers were more likely to seek their fortunes on
the rich lands of the western states or the British colonies
rather than in New England. But while departures from the
old country remained low through 1820–5, a belief was
growing among influential opinion-formers in Britain that
the country was becoming over-full of non-productive,
'redundant' population who were proving immensely ex-
pensive as they went onto poor relief. These were the vast
army of able-bodied poor who had had to go 'on the parish'
either because they had returned from the wars and found
no work or because the advent of industrial machinery had
wrecked their cottage industries and left them workless.
(The handloom weavers were probably the worst hit in the
latter way. Of course the then fashionable Malthusian
thinking asserted that behind unemployment was not a
complex of economic or social causes but the wilful idleness
of the able-bodied indigent.)

Men like Robert Wilmot Horton, in the Colonial Office
in 1827, had long been advocating assisted emigration as a
remedy for this embarrassing abundance, and the official
view soon came round to seeing emigration no longer as
the loss of a national resource but as a safety valve drain-
ing off a dangerous excess. So there grew up various state-
aided schemes for 'shovelling out paupers', with, naturally,
most of the shovelsful providing useful new settlements in
Canada or Australia. More importantly for the United
States, the new attitude to emigration smoothed the way
for *un*assisted emigrants. The government rescinded earlier
humanitarian regulations fixing the number of people to
be carried on emigrant ships and the quality of food, sanitation and so on aboard those ships. Ship owners rushed
to turn a quick profit, taking vessels carrying American
timber to Britan and altering them—with crudely built
bunks and little else—to carry the maximum number of
emigrants on the return journey. At the same time, most
crucially for New England, the long-standing laws governing who could or could not emigrate were repealed. So
the doors were thrown wide open to emigration, the means

—however frightful those timber ships might be—were available and comparatively cheap and there was, potentially, work and space and freedom to be had in America, for those who could manage the journey.

So the ripples of the 1820s became a definite wave in the 1830s, estimated at about 30,000 departures each year from the British Isles to the United States. The Irish bulked especially large among these arrivals—most of them farm labourers or unskilled workers fleeing from a poverty that was far more wretched than anything England or even Scotland had to show. Indeed, as many commentators noted, when the English or Scottish poor turned their backs on their misery and sailed out of Liverpool or Greenock, they passed boatloads of Irish pouring in through those ports to 'fill up every vacuum' as the poet laureate Robert Southey put it—and to call their new situation an improvement. English paupers also continued to leave, thanks to a Poor Law in 1834 allowing parishes to assist such departures from the rates: Kent was especially active in such shovellings out. But many other English arrivals at this time were the 'new aristocrats' of emigration, the skilled workmen, bringing their knowledge and experience to give a boost to American industry.

Clearly if there were such a thing as American or Yankee 'know-how' it included knowing how to get the experts working on Yankees' behalf. News went across the Atlantic of American wages—30 to 100 per cent higher than British—while it was said that a family of six which paid £17 a year in taxes in Britain would pay only the equivalent of thirty shillings in America. Of course the American cost of living was also proportionately higher, and America was (because of an insecure currency) especially susceptible to regular recessions and industrial cutbacks (1836–7 saw a particularly grim period). But English workers did not necessarily know that. They did know that America needed workers, while England—with a mounting unemployment rate—apparently did not. Recruiting agents sent over by American manufacturers made such points very clear, and scooped up quantities of workers—as when in 1837 a representative of a mill in Lowell, Mass., heard of unemployment in Uley, Gloucestershire, and gathered up half the complement of one broadcloth mill in that town. And these induced others to follow, by writing home stimu-

# STEAM TO
# Montreal, New York,
# Boston, &c.,
## VIA PORTLAND.

CANADIAN      STEAM

NAVIGATION      COMPANY.

THE STEAM SHIP

# SARAH SANDS,

### CAPTAIN W. ILSLEY,

## NOW LOADING IN BIRKENHEAD DOCKS,

WILL BE DESPATCHED FOR

# PORTLAND, U.S.

### On Monday, January 30th, 1854.

## RATE OF PASSAGE,

*Including Fare by Railway from Portland:—*

|  | First Cabin. | Second Cabin. | Third Class. | Including PROVISIONS Properly Cooked. |
|---|---|---|---|---|
| To MONTREAL | 20 Guineas. | 15 & 13 Guineas. | 7 Guineas. | |
| „ BOSTON - - | 20 Do. | 15 „ 13 Do. | 7 Do. | |
| „ NEW YORK | 20 Do. | 15 „ 13 Do. | 8 Do. | |

## RATE OF FREIGHT,

FROM LIVERPOOL,

*Including Carriage by Railway from Portland:—*

To BOSTON    - - -    **70s.** ℀ Ton Measurement, and 5 ℀ Cent. Primage.

„ NEW YORK ⎫
    OR     ⎬   - **80s.**    „    „    5 ℀ Cent. „
„ MONTREAL ⎭

    The Company's Steamers sail in conjunction with the Railways from Portland to ‾nada and the States. The Railway Cars run alongside the Steamers at Portland, and every facility is given for the transport of Passengers and Merchandize immediately on ‾rival. Apply to

## McKEAN, McLARTY & CO.
### Drury-lane, Water-street, Liverpool.

*Liverpool, 20th January, 1854.*

---

*A mid-nineteenth-century emigration poster from a steamship company: with a 7-guinea third-class rate to Boston via Portland, Maine*

lating accounts of life in America: 'We can have the taste of a piece of meat here, but when we were in England, looking at it was our share.'

Textiles as always received the lion's share of these new-comers, who tended to be mostly from Lancashire and Yorkshire (when they were not Scottish). But there were also miners from the Midlands, cutlers from Sheffield, metal workers and potters from Staffordshire and a host of other trades. Of course industry in New York and Pennsyl-vania claimed many; but for the 'artisans' of British in-dustry New England was becoming a primary magnet, as its youthful industrialization developed and spread, swell-ing the cities further—Boston's population doubled from 1820 to 1840, reaching 90,000—and throwing off manu-facturing 'new towns' around them, impressive complexes of factories as in the textile heartland of Lowell, Fall River, Lawrence, Webster and more.

A good many New Englanders fretted about this influx of strangers, but only rarely about those who brought price-less industrial skills. They objected to their states being a dumping ground for old-country paupers (in most Boston almshouses and the like in the 1830s immigrants out-numbered natives by about two to one). But others ob-jected on the grounds of the old racial and religious bigot-ries. The Irish were flowing into New England, to fill the vacuums there too, principally forming a huge pool of unskilled labour from which industry could draw. But the virulent Protestant hatred of 'papism' showed itself in a flurry of propaganda and rioting—as when a convent and girls' school in Charlestown was burned to the ground in the 1830s, fortunately, with no loss of life, by a mob of 4,000 Massachusetts Protestants. Such viciousness continued well into the 1840s, when New England and America gener-ally would feel in danger of being swamped by Catholicism, as successive failures of the potato crops drove Irishmen in their hundreds of thousands out of Ireland, with famine and pestilence at their heels.

And this emigration—the mightiest trans-Atlantic move-ment yet—was reflected and augmented in nearly every land. Scottish and English farmers had in previous years also turned readily to growing potatoes, which proved both more nourishing and more profitable than the grain crops then available. The blight destroyed their hopes through-

## Second Colonization

out Britain, and wreaked damage on the continent too. In the 1840s and 1850s, when the enormous tidal wave of migration to the New World reached its crest, nearly *four million* people chose to enter American ports—at a time when the entire population of the United States was only about twenty million.

Abject poverty, on a level where mere survival was an achievement, was the motive force of this mass movement. The British poor sold off their few pitiful possessions for the few shillings they needed for the fare, and crowded into the holds of the timber ships—starving, ragged, totally unprepared to 'begin anew' in America, and often diseased. Much has been written about the hellish nature of life below decks on the emigrant ships in those years, horrifyingly overcrowded until sufficient numbers had died en route to make room, putrid and pestilential in their lack of proper provisions, sanitation, even air. An American doctor in 1847 stepped reluctantly down into the 'steerage' section of a ship from Liverpool and wrote, appalled, about

> . . . the indescribable filth, the emaciated, half-nude figures, many with the eruption disfiguring their faces, crouching in their bunks or strewn over the decks. . . . Some were just rising from their berths for the first time since leaving Liverpool, having been suffered to lie there during the entire voyage wallowing in their own filth.

Naturally, as hinted in the doctor's reference to 'the eruption', disease ran riot in these conditions—typhus, smallpox, the scourge of cholera. Horror stories are told about the 'quarantine' areas set aside by the American authorities, to allow the epidemic to run its course through a hapless shipload of people, a cruel Darwinian attitude that afterwards grandly allowed the survivors, if any, to stumble into America. Massachusetts had its own way of blocking the entry of undesirables, which included the indigent as well as the ill: new laws demanded that ships' captains post a bond (when most strictly enforced it was $1,000 for *each* passenger) to guarantee that none should become a charge upon the local authority. Justification of this measure was found in the cost of poor relief: for instance, in 1847 some 2,000 out of 2,500 inmates of the

97

Boston Almshouse were foreign-born. But in any case the law meant that every voyage would be protracted, the landing delayed, while the ship's master looked for some port where enforcement was lax. And while he looked, his passengers died.

There is no adequate picture possible of the magnitude of this misery without a discussion of several volumes; these hints must suffice. Hints, too, should be given of the fact that for these wretched immigrants life in America did not often live up to their anticipation. Most of them congregated in the eastern cities, the seaports where they landed, because they lacked the means to move on. If they found work at all, it was the roughest manual work at exploitative wages—fifty cents for fifteen hours' labouring in the building trades and the like. And their desperate willingness to accept even this treatment did not endear them to native-born workers. With such incomes, too, the immigrants could not hope to gather the wherewithal to move on to the boom towns of the west, or even to improve their conditions in the east. A report by a Boston doctor, who had in 1849 taken an uncommonly close look at the urban poor, deserves excerpting:

> ... the dwellings of the poor are extremely filthy, often from neglect on the part of the occupants, as often from neglect on the part of the landlords, who get large rents, and do not provide suitable drains, privies, yards, etc. ... I have found from six to forty or more in one house of two stories, eleven and more in one room constantly, and eight in one bed (women and men).

Another report from 1849, from the Boston Committee of Internal Health, reinforced this dismal picture of 'wretched, dirty and unhealthy' houses in newly created slum areas, each of which was

> a perfect hive of human beings, without comforts and mostly without common necessaries; in many cases, huddled together like brutes, without regard to sex, or age, or sense of decency. ...

Other reports tell more about the unspeakable overcrowding—as when a newspaper reporter located one small house containing a shop, in part, with the remainder inhabited by exactly 120 persons, making up twenty-five families.

Working conditions were not much better: medical reports tell of mill girls in Lowell, Mass., who lived six or eight to a small room in company dormitories and who were packed by the dozen into not much larger rooms in the mill with the most primitive ventilation. Even worse was the situation of children in the New England factories: by 1831 the Rhode Island textile mills had about 3,500 children under twelve at work for ten to fourteen hours a day, six days a week, for about $1.50 a week. In 1842 Massachusetts legislators felt quite progressive when they forbade children under twelve to work more than ten hours a day. In short, the early Victorian industrial and urban horrors so well recorded by English writers were being repeated in America. The Statue of Liberty might soon be making her promises to Europe's 'huddled masses, yearning to breathe free', but there was not much of a tradition of free breathing being laid down in New England.

Again, however, the cream of the emigrants did not have to put up with such conditions: the skilled workers mostly from English manufacturing areas were desperately needed by industrial New England to keep the mills running and to bring in new techniques and machinery without which those industries could never have progressed and developed. Therefore the sensible mill owners made these valuable emigrants as happy as possible, offering company houses and other 'perks'. There were numerous artisans and other workers brought in under the system of 'contract labour', of course, when such concern for workers' happiness did not emerge. In that system the manufacturer paid the emigrant's passage and he contracted to work until the loan, with considerable interest and other additions, was paid off. Obviously, though, this system allowed much scope for abuse—by managers not fulfilling the promises of their propaganda, by workers vanishing into other parts of America upon their ships' arrival. Indeed, because of the abuses, Congress banned the contract-labour process in 1885. But just as often the shortage of skilled labour was so severe that the factory owners would pay workers' passage without contracts, as when in the early 1860s a group of Boston manufacturers formed an Emigrant Aid Society, pooling funds to gather 'mechanics' from Lancashire, Staffordshire and elsewhere. The owners of woollen mills in Webster were among those who quickly followed suit, until it seemed to be very much a sellers' market for any Englishman with skills, especially in textiles. And any would-be emigrants who could not find free passages that way tended to form their own emigration societies and pool their resources, as did Lancashire workers in the 1860s, when they were leaving at a rate of several dozen a week (fifty-one from Blackburn in one high-point week). Then, too, there were cases like that of the Nottingham *manufacturer*, in later years of the century, who emigrated to start a mill in Rhode Island and took 100 of his employees with him.

But the employers soon found that, in spite of the free passages and other inducements, not all of these English workmen seemed to be placid of nature or pathetically grateful. In fact, this emigration of skilled workers brought in wolves among the sheep. The New England mill owners had to face the fact that importing English industrial skills also meant importing British working-class radicalism. And it was in this role—rather than in quantity, for it was vastly outnumbered by the Irish and Continental European—that the English emigration made its biggest impact on America.

The radical tradition did not, of course, have to wait until mid-century to be transplanted to industrializing America. Years before, businessmen in New England as elsewhere had had glimpses of the uncomfortable fact that to import British workers usually meant bringing in the infection of trade unionism. For instance, in a famous case of the 1820s, a group of Scottish emigrant weavers in Thompsonville, Conn., were hauled into court by their employer on a charge of 'conspiracy' when they tried to form a union. Fortunately for the future of the American labour movement, the weavers were acquitted. Later, in the 1830s, a rapidly organized union with only transplanted Englishmen as members, called the Massachusetts Block Printers, achieved a then unheard-of success by getting the men's working hours reduced to ten a day.

The battle for the ten-hour day occupied much radical energy in the 1850s, when apparently employers tried to block the reform with any weapon possible—not only the threat of discharge but the threat of eviction from company dwellings, court action to reclaim passage money advanced to immigrants and so on. Such pressures and employer disciplines were behind the action of a group of Sheffield cutlers, emigrants to Waterbury, Conn., in the late 1830s, who in 1852 picked up and moved to New York where they began a co-operative, worker-controlled factory. But that was a fairly unusual reaction to the struggle for improved working conditions—a struggle, as it happened, that generally failed until later decades, so that in the 1860s the textile mills of Massachusetts still ran a minimum eleven hours a day, six days a week. (And the individual workers in the mills worked harder, managing more machines than would have been the case in England—eight looms for every weaver, for instance, as opposed to four.)

Still, in spite of failures, something like the good fight was fought over the years by the English emigrant workers —especially by the Chartists among them. These radical reformers, whose influence was strongest in industrial areas of England, had been for some time the activist spearhead of Britain's struggling trade-union movement. Though at first they actively opposed emigration—calling it the 'transportation of the innocent' and a management technique to weaken working-class unity—eventually Chartist leaders began to find value in it. A few idealistically saw in the American Constitution a model of their social-democratic dreams; other Chartists left Britain in a weary belief that she was socially and politically incorrigible; and the 'direct action' sector of the movement left in headlong flight from the authorities who sought to imprison them for subversion after waves of rioting in the early 1840s. Up to 1848 the British persecution of Chartists and other radicals strengthened considerably—a contemporary comment says they were 'hunted like wild beasts'—and so the emigrant passenger lists included some notable Chartist names. Among them was James Dillon, a shoemaker from Stockport in Cheshire, who emigrated to Massachusetts in 1845 and who in 1860 organized the Lynn shoemakers in what has been called 'the greatest strike in American history before the Civil War'. Some 20,000 workers walked out that year, stayed out for more than two months, and finally wrested from about thirty manufacturers a wage rise of about 10 per cent. There was also W. J. Linton, Chartist theorist and editor of *The English Republic,* who managed to escape the official wrath that followed the revolutionary fire of the late 1840s by retiring to Cumberland, and who later quietly made his way to New Haven.

It should be added that many of the Chartist emigrants did not stay long—in the manner of Feargus O'Connor, the major leader, who visited America briefly while waiting for the pursuit in Britain to cool. Some grew homesick and went back; others grew disillusioned. A Lanarkshire compositor and Chartist, William S. Brown, who emigrated in the 1850s after serving a term in prison for his political activities, wrote disappointedly from Boston that 'universal suffrage is *not* producing many of the fruits predicted of it in the old country'. One of the fruits that was certainly not being produced a few years later was any true acknowledgement of human equality: with the rest of the world, the Chartists in America watched in horror as the Union prepared to tear itself apart in civil war over whether some men could hold others in slavery.

When that exercise in self-destruction had been concluded, it seems that the labour movement took up the good fight where it left off. Historians have noted that the pre-Civil-War struggle had been mostly defensive; in the 1870s it turned to aggression, prompting outraged response from employers—especially against the danger from the English agitator in their midst:

> Communist, socialist, molly maguire, incendiary, blood and thunder spouter, hungry looking loafer, a sinister faced wretch whose company could be dispensed with in this community. . . .

Most remarkable were the waves of major strikes in the Fall River area of Massachusetts in the 1870s, with Lancashire millworkers prominent among the fire-eaters—'very much indisposed to submit to injustice', as a contemporary account put it, 'prompt to contend for what they consider their right'. A Lancashire man, George Gunton, edited the *Labor Standard* after emigrating in 1874, and was indeed the standard-bearer in Fall River. He and other Massachusetts Englishmen also contributed to the political battle for the ten-hour day, which bore fruit in legislation passed in 1874 in Massachusetts, later extended to other states.

## Second Colonization

The shocks and torments of the War Between the States had not greatly affected the movement of Britons to New England—indeed, may have enhanced it. The Union army claimed so many industrial workers that replacements had to be brought in; more importantly, the blockade of the south brought a 'cotton famine' to Lancashire and elsewhere in England's industrial north, and the resulting stoppages sent thousands of unemployed mill workers to America, often with aid from their unions. Then, in post-war years, the new expansion of American industry drew even more workers, in a steady if otherwise unremarkable flow. It is clear that Fall River and nearby areas might well have been renamed New Lancashire, while in Lawrence and the wool areas visitors noted that even native-born American workers had picked up the Yorkshire dialect. So, too, Sheffield craftsmen were still thick on the ground in Connecticut in the 1870s; West Country stone cutters laboured in the expanding quarries of Maine, New Hampshire and Vermont; English artisans of every sort thronged the building trades that were transforming Boston and the other centres into cities that could fairly enter the twentieth century. As late as 1903, a British visitor could assert

> that America even today is largely dependent upon British-trained skilled labour in almost every department of industry.

As regards America generally, English immigration increased notably through the 1870s, lying third behind the German and Scandinavian. But this movement—not all industrial and not at all homogenous—reached its peak in the 1880s and thereafter began to dwindle. It was soon overtaken again by the Irish, and then by a new development—the arrival of hordes from Russia, the Austro-Hungarian empire, Italy, Greece and elsewhere in eastern and southern Europe. By the mid-1890s this immigration would have swollen to nearly 80 per cent of the total immigration into America, and would swell further still in the early years of the new century. In those years the movement into America of British emigrants would have dropped away to comparative negligibility.

# The English to New England

Certainly before then the movement of the English to New England, specifically, would have faded to near vanishing point. Those states kept up their tradition of pioneering restlessness, sending out waves of their own emigrants into the hugely expanding American west. And, frequently, second-generation English, Irish or German New Englanders also followed this process, making room in the factories or on the farms for the newest newcomers—Hungarians, Italians, Poles, Greeks, some Portuguese, a sizeable community of French Canadians. These were the sort of 'foreigners' who stirred up the bigotries of white Anglo-Saxon Protestant America—reinforced by that usual Yankee exclusiveness and xenophobia which had long characterized New England.

So the New England cities became hotbeds of 'nativism', in the tradition of Boston's anti-Catholic, anti-immigrant 'Know Nothings' of the 1850s, a pressure group that had tried to create legislative restriction against immigration, but that had faded after some political setbacks and with the build-up to the Civil War. Now, in new guises, the 'America for Americans' approach took hold again, accompanied by considerable violence and some terrorism aimed at the new European arrivals. Perhaps the flowering of these hatreds once again damaged New England's image for British emigrants; but perhaps also the presence of so many 'foreigners' served as a deterrent for many Englishmen. But if these factors contributed at all to the diminution of English emigration to New England, they did so only minutely. The English emigrant then was what he still is—not part of a mass movement but a person leaving his homeland as an individual or with his family for the purpose of bettering himself in one or another land of opportunity. And New England at that time had little to offer him, in comparison with the fertile California valleys, the free homesteads of western Canada, the rich grazing lands of Australia. New England was industrialized, urbanized, over-populated; its rural areas were cramped, less than fertile, thoroughly occupied; its industrial areas were squalid, grimy, turbulent, polyglot and aswarm. The wide-open spaces and opportunities of the colonies were clearly far more inviting.

Yet however increasingly small was the English share of the population, England and Englishness continued to

Second Colonization

exercise a disproportionate and almost mystical influence over life in the north-eastern states. Englishness and Puritanism and all the elements of New England's colonial past came together into a huge and perhaps burdensome heritage. New Englanders remembered that the first people to bear that name thought of themselves as something of a 'chosen people', under a special divine providence; the Yankee descendants of the Puritans continued to view themselves as different from the rest of America, and generally superior within that difference. The superiority lay in realms such as adherence to the generally accepted moral values—most of them reflecting the Puritan ethic, hard work and thrift and godliness and the like. In these matters New England tended to be very much facing towards the old world and the old ways; and so it did in a perhaps more tangible area where its sense of superiority was directly linked with the English heritage. This was the sudden nascence of a native American cultural, educational and literary tradition which could hold up its head in any company, and which grew principally in New England, with men like Emerson, Thoreau and Hawthorne as principal fructifying figures. The poet James Russell Lowell could speak out against his contemporaries, however, as writers who 'steal Englishmen's books and think Englishmen's thoughts'. And certainly it would be some time before New England writers did not frequently look over their shoulders for guidelines and approbation from London.

Of course there are innumerable other areas within which one might generalize about the continuing Englishness of New England—even on the level of all the old jokes about the tradition-haunted, ancestor-worshipping family snobbery based on *Mayflower* antecedents. Above all, the people of New England felt themselves (and probably still do) somehow to be a repository of a kind of original virtue, which permeates all the foundations of the American nation. And for them, this virtue was an importation from England. In a way it seems that the whole country came to agree with this view, when the mythologizing of the New England past became complete. So, for instance, all America sits down to a ceremonial feast on the anniversary called Thanksgiving (established by Lincoln); so all America on the fourth of July recalls or re-enacts revolutionary excitements like the ride of Paul Revere. It seems, then, that

## The English to New England

America has taken to itself the parochial Puritans of Massachusetts as the ancestral figures of the entire nation. Few other emigrations, so limited within physical space, have managed to reach so far.

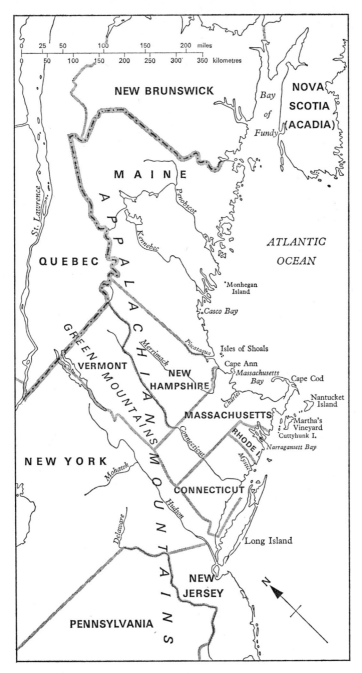

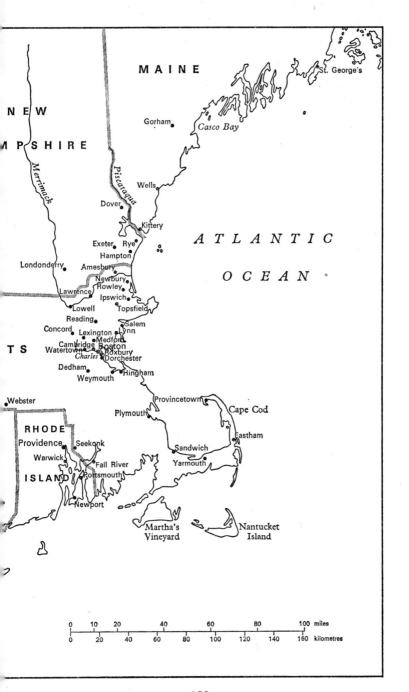

MAINE

St. George's

NEW

MPSHIRE

*Merrimack*

*Piscataqua*

Gorham

*Casco Bay*

Wells

Dover

Kittery

Exeter  Rye

Hampton

Londonderry

Amesbury

Newbury

Rowley

Lawrence

Ipswich

Lowell

Topsfield

Reading

Salem

Concord

Lexington  Lynn

Medford

Cambridge  Boston

Watertown  Roxbury

*Charles*  Dorchester

Dedham

Hingham

Weymouth

*ATLANTIC*

*OCEAN*

Webster

Provincetown

Plymouth

Cape Cod

RHODE

Eastham

Providence

Seekonk

Warwick

Sandwich

Fall River

Yarmouth

ISLAND

Portsmouth

Newport

Martha's
Vineyard

Nantucket
Island

| 0 | 10 | 20 | | 40 | | 60 | | 80 | | 100 miles |
| 0 | 20 | 40 | 60 | 80 | 100 | 120 | 140 | 160 kilometres |

# Selected Bibliography

ABBOTT, Edith, *Immigration* (Chicago, 1924)

ABBOTT, Edith, *Historical Aspects of the Immigration Problem* (Chicago, 1926)

ADAMS, James Truslow, *The Founding of New England; Revolutionary New England; New England in the Republic* (Boston, 1921–7)

ANDREWS, C. M., *Beginnings of Connecticut* (New Haven, 1934)

ANDREWS, C. M., *The Colonial Period of American History* (4 vols) (New Haven, London, 1936–8)

BANKS, C. E., *The Winthrop Fleet of 1630* (Boston, 1930)

BARCK, O. T., and LEFLER, H. T., *Colonial America* (New York, London, 1968)

BEARDSLEY, F. G., *Builders of a Nation* (Boston, 1921)

BERTHOFF, Rowland T., *British Immigrants in Industrial America* (Cambridge, Mass., 1953)

BOLTON, Charles K., *The Real Founders of New England* (Boston, 1929)

BOLTON, Ethel S., *Immigrants to New England* (Baltimore, 1966)

BOORSTIN, Daniel J., *The Americans: the Colonial Experience* (New York, 1958)

BOSTON, Ray, *British Chartists in America* (Manchester, New Jersey, 1971)

BRADFORD, William, *History of Plymouth Plantation*, ed. William T. Davis (New York, 1908)

BURRAGE, H. S., *Beginnings of Colonial Maine* (Portland, Me., 1914)

BUSHMAN, Richard L., *From Puritan to Yankee* (Cambridge, Mass., 1967)

CALDER, I. M., *New Haven Colony* (New Haven, 1934)

CAMPBELL, Mildred, 'English Emigration on the Eve of the American Revolution', *American Historical Review* (October, 1955)

CARROLL, Charles, *Rhode Island* (4 vols) (New York, 1932)

CARROTHERS, W. A., *Emigration from the British Isles* (London, 1929)

# Selected Bibliography

CLARK, George L., *History of Connecticut* (New York, London, 1914)

COLEMAN, Peter J., *Transformation of Rhode Island* (Providence, R. I., 1963)

CRAVEN, W. F., *Colonies in Transition* (New York, 1968)

DEMOS, John, *A Little Commonwealth* (New York, 1970)

DOW, G. F., *Every Day Life in the Massachusetts Bay Colony* (Boston, 1935)

DOYLE, J. A., *The English in America* ('Puritan Colonies', 2 vols) (London, 1887)

DUNN, R. S., *Puritans and Yankees* (Princeton, 1962)

ERICKSON, Charlotte, *American Industry and the European Immigrant* (Cambridge, Mass., 1957)

ERICKSON, Charlotte, *Invisible Immigrants* (London, 1972)

GILL, Crispin, *Mayflower Remembered* (Newton Abbot, Devon, 1970)

GOETZMANN, William H. (ed.), *The Colonial Horizon* (Reading, Mass., 1969)

GUTMAN, Judith M., *The Colonial Venture* (New York, 1966)

HANDLIN, Oscar (ed.), *Immigration as a Factor in American History* (New York, 1959)

HANDLIN, Oscar, *Boston's Immigrants* (Cambridge, Mass., 1941)

HANSEN, Marcus L., *Atlantic Migration* (Cambridge, Mass., 1941)

HANSEN, Marcus L., *The Immigrant in American History* (Cambridge, Mass., 1942)

HART, A. B. (ed.), *The Commonwealth History of Massachusetts* (5 vols) (New York, 1927–30)

HAWKE, David, *The Colonial Experience* (New York, 1966)

HOWE, Henry F., *Prologue to New England* (New York, 1943)

JAMES, B. B. *Colonisation of New England* (Philadelphia, 1904)

JAMES, Sydney V. (ed.), *The New England Puritans* (New York, 1968)

JENNINGS, John E., *Boston, Cradle of Liberty* (New York, 1947)

JOHNSON, Edward, *Wonder Working Providence*, ed. J. F. Jameson (New York, 1906)

JOHNSON, Stanley C., *A History of Emigration from the United Kingdom to North America* (London, 1913)

JONES, Maldwyn Allen, *American Immigration* (Chicago, 1960)

KINNEY, Charles B., *Church and State . . . in New Hampshire* (New York, 1955)

KRAUS, Michael, *Immigration: the American Mosaic* (Princeton, 1966)

KRAUS, Michael, *North Atlantic Civilisation* (Princeton, 1957)

LANGDON, G. D., *Pilgrim Colony* (New Haven, 1966)

# Selected Bibliography

LEACH, D. E., *Flintlock and Tomahawk* (New York, 1958)

LORD, Arthur, *Plymouth and the Pilgrims* (Boston, New York, 1920)

MARBLE, Annie R., *The Women Who Came in the Mayflower* (Boston, Chicago, 1920)

MATHEWS, Lois, K., *The Expansion of New England* (New York, 1962)

McCLINTOCK, J. N., *History of New Hampshire* (Boston, 1889)

MILLER, Perry, *From Colony to Province* (Cambridge, Mass., 1953)

MORGAN, Edmund S. (ed.), *The Founding of Massachusetts* (Indianapolis, 1964)

MORGAN, Forrest, *Connecticut as a Colony and as a State* (4 vols) (Hartford, Conn., 1904)

NETTELS, C. P., *The Roots of American Civilisation* (second edition) (New York, 1964)

OSGOOD, H. L., *The American Colonies in the Eighteenth Century* (4 vols) (New York, 1924)

PALFREY, J. G., *History of New England* (4 vols) (Boston, 1858–75)

SCOTT, Franklin D., *Emigration and Immigration* (New York, 1963)

SHEPPERSON, W. S., *British Emigration to North America* (Oxford, 1957)

SHIPTON, C. K., 'Immigration to New England 1680–1740', *Journal of Political Economy* (April 1936)

SIMPSON, Alan, *Puritanism in Old and New England* (Chicago, 1955)

SMITH, Richmond Mayo, *Emigration and Immigration* (London, 1890)

SOLOMON, Barbara M., *Ancestors and Immigrants* (Cambridge, Mass., 1956)

STARKEY, Marion L., *Land Where Our Fathers Died* (London, 1964)

THOMPSON, C. M., *Independent Vermont* (Boston, 1942)

TYLER, L. G., *England in America* (New York, 1930)

VAUGHAN, Alden T., *New England Frontier* (Boston, 1965)

WARD, Harry M., *United Colonies of New England* (New York, 1961)

WERTENBAKER, T. J., *Puritan Oligarchy* (New York, 1947)

WILLISON, George F., *Saints and Strangers* (London, 1946)

WINSLOW, Ola E., *Master Roger Williams* (New York, 1957)

WINTHROP, John, *Journal*, ed. J. K. Hosmer (New York, 1906)

WRIGHT, Louis B., *The Atlantic Frontier* (New York, 1959)

WRIGHT, Louis B., and FOWLER, E. W. (eds.), *English Colonisation of North America* (London, 1968)

YEARLEY, C. K., *Britons in American Labour* (Baltimore, 1957)

# Index

# Index

Concord, Mass., 45, 83
Congress, 83, 99
Connecticut, 2, 46, 48, 49, 53, 54, 56, 58, 60, 61 62, 63, 65, 69, 71, 74, 75, 76, 85, 86, 91, 103; Fundamental Orders of, 50; river, 47, 48
Constitution, 91, 101
Cooper, Fenimore, 46
Cornwall, 3
Cotton, John, 39, 49, 52, 64
Council for New England, 28, 29, 31, 36, 37, 47, 54, 55
Cowes, I. of W., 39
Craddock, Matthew, 38
Crèvecoeur, de, 88
Cromwell, Oliver, 49, 69
Cumberland, 102
Cuttyhunk, 4

Darwin, Charles, 97
Davenport, John, 53-4
Dedham, Mass., 45
Delaware, 77
Devon, 4, 5
Dillon, James, 101
Dominion of New England, 74
Dorchester, Dorset, 36
Dorchester, Mass., 45, 47
Dover, N. H., 55
Dutch settlements, 30, 46, 47, 48, 61, 63, 71, 74
Dyer, Mary, 65f.

East Anglia, 39
Eastham, Mass., 63
Eaton, Theophilus, 54
Emerson, Ralph Waldo, 83, 90, 105
Emigrant Aid Society, 100
Empire Loyalists, 86
Endecott, John, 36f., 41, 57, 64, 66
England, 2, 4, 15, 26, 27, 28, 30, 47, 48, 55, 56, 61, 65, 74, 75, 76f., 87, 88f., 101, 102, 103, 104; Civil War, 61; and Puritans, 33f., 56, 60f., 66, 72, 74
Exeter, N. H., 55

Fall River, Mass., 95, 102, 103
*Fortune*, 26
Fox, George, 64
France, 2, 5, 26, 29, 75-6, 80, 81, 87, 88; colonies, 61, 63, 74; emigration from, 75, 77-8, 79
Frontenac, 76
fur trading, 2

General Court of Massachusetts, 37, 43, 57, 60
George III, 77, 81
Georgia, 77, 85
Germany, 78, 87, 103, 104
Gilbert, Raleigh, 3, 6, 7; Sir Humphrey, 3; Sir John, 7
Gloucestershire, 39
Goetzmann, William H., 33
Goffe, William, 69
Gomez, Estevan, 3
Gorges, Robert, 29, 36; Sir Ferdinando, 5, 6, 10-11, 28, 29, 36, 54, 55, 56, 71
Gorham, Maine, 80
Gorton, Samuel, 53
Gosnold, Bartholomew, 3, 4, 6, 7
Grand Banks, 2
Greece, 103, 104
Green Mountain Boys, 85
Greenock, Scotland, 93
Greenwich, England, 80
Guilford, Conn., 54
Gunton, George, 102

Hakluyt, Richard, 1, 2, 3
Halifax, Lord, 81
Hampton, N. H., 55
Hartford, Conn., 48, 50, 88
Hartley, Jonathan, 79
Harvard College, 71
Hawthorne, Nathaniel, 105
Higginson, Francis, 37
Hilton brothers, 55
Hingham, Mass., 45
Holland, 12f., 17, 31, 75
Hooker, Thomas, 49, 50, 64

# Index

# Index

Newfoundland, 2, 3, 79
New Hampshire, 2, 4, 29, 54, 55, 69, 71, 73-4, 75, 78, 80, 85, 103; Grants, 85
New Haven, Conn., 54, 62, 65, 69, 102
New Jersey, 6, 28-9, 74
New Meadows, *see* Topsfield
New London, Conn., 63
New Plymouth, *see* Plymouth
Newport, R.I., 53
Newton, *see* Cambridge
New York, 30, 71, 74, 78, 80, 85, 86, 87, 95, 101
Norfolk 45, 55
Northamptonshire, 39
Northwest Passage, 2
Norwalk, Conn., 63
Nottingham, Notts., 100

O'Connor, Feargus, 102
Ohio, 83, 86
Oldham, John, 46, 57-8
Ottawa Indians, 81

Passamaquoddy Bay, 6
Patuxet, 24
Penn, William, 77
Pennsylvania, 77, 78, 86, 88, 95
Penobscot river, 9
Pequot Indians, 46, 47, 57-8, 59, 63; War, 64, 72
Philadelphia, Penn., 87
Pilgrims, 12-31 passim, 41, 43f., 47, 48, 53f., 65-8
Piscataqua river, 55, 71
Pitt, William, 81
Plains of Abraham, 81
Plant, Matthias, 80
Plymouth, Devon, 15, 29, 46
Plymouth, Mass., 5, 6, 20, 24, 27, 28, 29, 30, 31, 35f., 46, 47, 50, 55, 57, 62, 65, 71, 72, 74, 75; Company, 6, 7, 10-11, 26, 28
Pocahontas, 9
Poland, 104
Pontiac, 81
Poor Law of 1834, 93

Popham, George, 6, 7; Sir John, 6
Portsmouth, R.I., 53
Portugal, 104
Presbyterianism, 78
Priestley, Joseph, 87-8
Pring, Martin, 4-5, 6
Providence Plantations, 62
Provincetown, Mass., 18, 19, 21, 25
Puritans, 11, 12, 33-56 passim, 57f., 64f., 69, 71, 73, 74f., 77, 78, 79, 91

Quakers, 64f., 77, 78
Quebec, 3; Act, 83
Quinnipiac Bay, 54

Radcliff, Jane, 79
Raleigh, Sir Walter, 3, 6
Randolph, Edward, 73
Reading, Mass., 45
Restoration, 66, 69
Revere, Paul, 105
Rhineland, 78
Rhode Island, 2, 53, 56, 62, 63, 64, 65, 69, 71, 77, 84, 85, 89, 91, 99, 100; Charter, 70, 74, 75
Roanoke Island, 3
Rowley, Mass., 45
Roxbury, Mass., 45
Royal Commission of 1664, 71-2
Russia, 103
Rye, N.H., 29

St. George's Harbour, 5
St. Lawrence river, 5, 76
Salem, Mass., 36, 40, 42, 44, 45, 51, 64
Saltonstall, Sir Richard, 38, 47, 48, 64, 77
Samoset, 24
Sandwich, Mass., 45
Saunders, 80
Saybrook, Conn., 48, 50
Saye and Sele, Lord, 48, 61

# Index